/

HUNTING
THE DEVIL

Hunting the Devil

Richard Lourie

HarperCollins*Publishers*

HarperCollins books may be purchased for educational, business, or sales promotional use. For information please write: Special Markets Department, HarperCollins Publishers, Inc., 10 East 53rd Street, New York, NY 10022.

FIRST EDITION

Designed by Claudyne Bianco

LIBRARY OF CONGRESS CATALOG CARD NUMBER 92-54729

ISBN 0-06-017717-9

93 94 95 96 97 HC 10 9 8 7 6 5 4 3 2 1

To

Edward Burlingame,
for being an editor of honor and intelligence,
Berenice Hoffman,
for seeing what isn't there,
Jod, for her support and patience, other names for love.

A WORD FROM THE AUTHOR

All the material in this book is taken from the official record and the recollections of participants. The principal documents are the indictment, the 225 volumes of evidence, the transcripts or interrogations as well as the audio- and videocassettes of them, the findings of the Serbsky Psychiatric Institute, and police photographs.

The portrait of Chikatilo derives directly from official documents, Chikatilo's own writings, and my observations of him at his trial. Here, I am principally indebted to Chief Inspector Issa Kostoev for sharing with me to the fullest his experience of the hunt for Chikatilo and of the seventeen days of interrogation when they were alone together. He was equally generous in speaking of his own twenty-seven years as an investigator, describing in depth the cases he had solved, touching on everything from strategy to slang. Inspector Yandiev was also forthcoming with his memories and insights as he escorted me from murder site to murder site.

Many people in Rostov took the time to initiate me into the lore of their city. Yana Tsulaya and Lyonya Grigorian helped me see what is always invisible to the outsider. Believing that no one could have a feel for Rostov without some sense of its river, Natasha Sotnikova and Yura Fadeev arranged for their Cossack friend, Shura, to take me in his outboard motorboat down the Don, where we observed tradition by drinking vodka in the river's honor.

The descriptions of people and places in this book are based on my own impressions and observations except in the obvious instances. Since I was not able to attend every day of Chikatilo's trial, I have at some points relied on newspaper accounts or those of spectators. While strictly adhering to known facts and chronology, I have of course used narrative devices in the attempt to catch the grit and fever of life. And no tale set in Russia would be true without excursions into the past, every story an old story in that land.

Every section of the population has been through the terrible sickness caused by terror, and none has so far recovered, or become fit again for normal civic life. It is an illness that is passed on to the next generation, so that the sons pay for the sins of the fathers and perhaps only the grandchildren begin to get over it—or at least it takes on a different form with them.

NADEZHDA MANDELSTAM, *Hope Against Hope*

And therefore, since I cannot prove a lover . . .
I am determined to prove a villain.

WILLIAM SHAKESPEARE, *King Richard III*

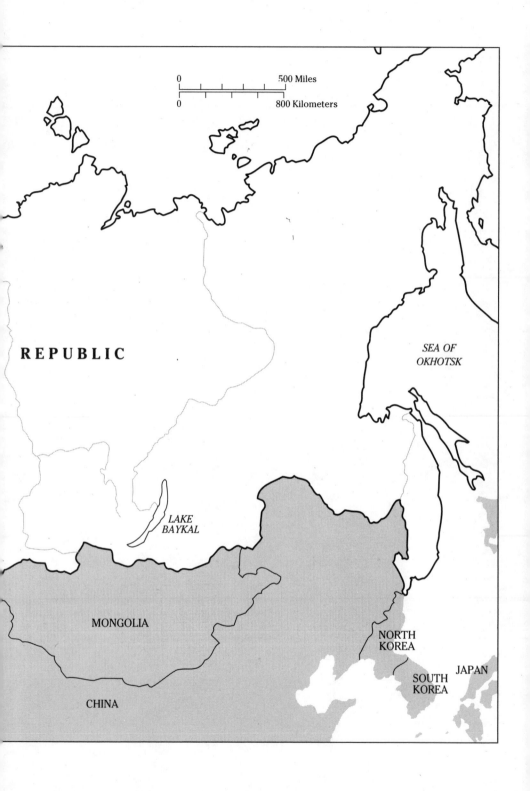

0   500 Miles

0   800 Kilometers

REPUBLIC

SEA OF OKHOTSK

LAKE BAYKAL

MONGOLIA

NORTH KOREA

JAPAN

SOUTH KOREA

CHINA

PROLOGUE

hief Inspector Kostoev checked the interrogation room one more time before the prisoner arrived. It was just the way he liked it, bare. There was only one picture on the wall, that of the KGB's founder, Feliks Dzerzhinsky, goateed, alert. There was a safe which hinted at secrets; let the prisoner imagine just what. There was the desk at which Inspector Kostoev would sit and, perpendicular to it, a table, forming a T. The prisoner would sit in the inside corner of the T, to Kostoev's right.

There would be nothing to look at but Kostoev. And even if the prisoner did look over at the safe or the picture, that was all to the good. They would remind him where he was, not in some jail in the sticks but in a KGB prison in the city of Rostov on the Don.

After a bitter fight with the Rostov police, who wanted custody, Inspector Kostoev of the Russian Republic's Attorney General's Office had won the right to have his prisoner remanded to the KGB prison. Although it was not customary for the Attorney General's Office to work with the KGB, Kostoev had sound reasons for breaching usual procedure. He did not want the prisoner to have any grounds to complain later of ill treatment. Some of the thirty-six women and children the prisoner was suspected of murdering and sexually cannibalizing had relatives on the Rostov police force. Kostoev wanted him isolated, beyond the reach of vengeance.

The prisoner was led through the corridors of the KGB prison in the time-honored way. The guard escorting him rapped his keys against his belt buckle to alert other guards in other corridors that a prisoner was coming. The prisoner was to see no one. And no one was to see the prisoner.

Slope-shouldered, with thinning sandy gray hair, the prisoner walked with a slow, almost elderly shuffle, his muscular, elongated neck thrust forward. He was a tall man with large hands; the middle finger on the right hand was bandaged. He looked like what he was—a low-level industrial engineer, a devoted reader of newspapers, a grandfather.

Inspector Kostoev had scarcely slept in the three days before the arrest. And every time he did fall asleep he would see the face of the man who was now being brought to him. But it had not been only anxiety and excitement that had kept Kostoev awake. As always, there were the most practical of reasons. Those would be the only days he would have to prepare himself for the duel that is interrogation.

For three days Inspector Kostoev had paced back and forth in Room 339 of the Hotel Rostov, where he had been living for years. A dapper, mustached man of forty-eight who carried himself grandly when out in the world, he was now oblivious to everything but the task at hand. He never left the room. Nothing registered if he looked out the window. Every minute had to be put to a single use—finding a way, as he always put it, "of getting inside the suspect's soul," to know his logic, hopes, and deepest fears.

Only in three cases out of the hundreds he had handled had he failed to obtain a confession. And those, of course, were the easiest to remember.

But he had never questioned a suspect like the man who

was on his way from the cell to him now. As chief of the Department for Crimes of Special Importance, murder was Inspector Kostoev's daily bread, but usually those were acts committed by professional criminals or by people who had succumbed to greed or rage. He had never before encountered a grandfather who maimed and murdered. Exactly what strategy did you use to get inside the soul of a family-man cannibal?

The tension had become unbearable on those overcast days in November while the suspect was still being tailed. Anything could go wrong. The Rostov police had proved uncountable times how unreliable they could be. At that stage as well, he could have requested the assistance of the KGB, who were masters of invisible surveillance, but it would have taken time to put a special request through the bureaucracy and time was one of the many things Inspector Kostoev did not have.

If the police were in the least unprofessional and the suspect became aware of them, he might slip away and hang himself or leap in front of a speeding trolley car. And there was nothing in all the world that Inspector Kostoev desired more than the good health of this man he knew to be a killer.

His certainty was as strong as his evidence was scant. And for that reason Inspector Kostoev had needed every second at his disposal to devise a strategy that would ensure success within the ten days of interrogation granted by law after the arrest of a suspect. Success meant a confession that could be substantiated; failure meant watching a murderer walk free.

Then, after three fitful days and three sleepless nights, Inspector Kostoev grunted to himself as he always did when a difficult problem had at last yielded to his mind and will. He knew what his strategy would be, and he knew it was right, for it was every bit as perverse as the suspect himself.

On November 19, 1990, he had obtained an arrest warrant for the following day, a Tuesday. Kostoev knew that he had a distinct disadvantage—the man had been arrested before, in 1984. The first arrest can be a great shock. It can stun a man and start a hairline fracture in the mind that interrogation can then jimmy open. Now the blow would be softened by a layer of experience. Still, if the arrest were sudden and swift, if the men chosen were reliable and could be counted on to maintain their silence, the prisoner's nerves might still get a good rattling. Even disadvantages had to be put to best use.

The suspect had been arrested on November 20, 1990, in the town of Novocherkassk where he resided. Three plainclothesmen had approached him on the sidewalk, asked him to identify himself, then handcuffed him and seated him in their car without saying another word, as Kostoev had instructed.

It is about twenty-five miles from Novocherkassk to the single block-long building on Engels Street in Rostov on the Don which houses both the police and the KGB, though each organization has separate entrances, separate wings, separate tasks. The road is straight and flat—this is steppe country. Barely visible in the distance on that rainy day were tall stands of trees, mostly poplars and acacias. Planted in rectangular patterns in the late forties under Stalin, these "forest strips" were designed to retain snow and runoff, preventing erosion. There had been so many murders in them that the hunt for the killer had become known as "Operation Forest Strip." Now that eight-year-long operation was coming to an end if the man in the back seat was indeed the killer. The police who made the arrest could not be sure. They did not know what, if anything, Kostoev knew. All they could do was follow orders and maintain silence as the car sped past the steppe, the stands of trees now merging with the rainy November dark.

The prisoner was meant to know that their silence was not accidental. That silence was a message to him from Inspector Kostoev—it was no secret he was the man in charge. And the message was—your case is of special importance.

But silence also gave a prisoner the chance to think, to prepare his position, to second-guess his opponent. And so that meant that the silence of the police had another meaning as well—it was a signal of Kostoev's confidence: Let the prisoner prepare all he wants.

Still handcuffed, he had been hustled into police headquarters on Engels Street in Rostov. Then he was photographed—full length, close-up, profile, full face, turn left, turn right.

Leaning slightly forward on the balls of his feet as if about to pounce, Kostoev watched the prisoner with unwavering eyes. Kostoev's voice boomed with shock waves of confidence, his questions not inquiries but commands to answer.

"Name?"

"Andrei Chikatilo."

"Date of birth?"

"October 16, 1936."

"Place of birth?"

"Ukraine. Village of Yablochnoye."

"Nationality?"

"Ukrainian."

"Education?"

"Rostov University, literature."

"Party member?"

"Expelled from party."

Chikatilo paused, stumbled, took deep breaths. But there was nothing unusual about that, and for the most part he was calm.

"What year were you married?"

"Nineteen sixty something, I don't remember, sixty something."

Now it was Kostoev who paused. A man who was truly innocent might suddenly forget when he was married, ashamed by the thought of his wife knowing he'd been in jail. But marriage might also be a sensitive point for a sexual murderer.

"Place of work?" barked Kostoev, returning to himself after an instant's distraction of insight. After the first answer, Kostoev had made Chikatilo list every place he had worked for the last twenty years. Where else, where else, where else?

The most important thing now was to impress Chikatilo with the force and caliber of the man he was up against. Kostoev knew his worth and wasn't afraid to flaunt it, especially if it could serve as good a purpose as intimidating the suspect.

Not that the suspect seemed intimidated yet, a little stunned, a little confused, but hardly in terror for his secrets, as he was led away into a big booming room where heads and cameras turned toward him, even the manual typewriter ceasing its clatter for a moment.

After the strip search and the doctor's questions—Kostoev off to the side now but his eyes never leaving the prisoner—Chikatilo had requested that interrogation not begin until the next day as he was feeling poorly. Kostoev had granted the request.

The guard had not come for Chikatilo until well after three in the afternoon. Was that too a sign of Kostoev's confidence—he could only hold him for ten days yet was willing to lose almost the entire first day?

Inspector Kostoev may have caught the approaching rap of keys on a buckle. In any case, Chikatilo would arrive in a minute or two. Though he had barked at him yesterday, he would be unfailingly polite today. The shock phase was over. Now it was time for interrogation, the most dangerous game of all, played by two, alone in a bare room, the stakes freedom or death.

No force would be used. No hint of threat. There would be nothing physical. This was a KGB interrogation room, a place where spirit met spirit.

PART I

C H A P T E R   1

She didn't like the look of it. What was that man trying to talk that little girl into? Why was he whispering to her? Why did he keep looking around like that?

The man and the little girl were about fifteen feet away from her at the trolley stop and she couldn't hear what they were saying. But she could keep her eye on them. Svetlana Gurenkova was a good citizen and, as a citizen, had the right and duty to take a hard look at anything that felt wrong to her.

The man was tall and big, but very slope-shouldered in his black overcoat. The face beneath his brown beaver-lamb fur cap was long, as was his nose. But it was hard to get an exact read on his features because his oversized glasses seemed to deflect her sight. In his forties, maybe fifty. He was carrying a shopping bag as most Soviets did in case they chanced upon anything interesting for sale. What had interested the man was a bottle of wine whose neck Svetlana could see protruding from the bag.

It was an unsavory combination, an older man, a bottle of wine, a chubby girl who couldn't have been more than ten. The girl was wearing a red coat whose hood was trimmed in black fur. But the hood was down. As better protection against the cold, the girl had on a rabbit-fur cap, dark brown like her eyes. Her face was oval and a touch simple but with fine, arched eyebrows and a high forehead. She was wearing a scarf. Either her mother had dressed her well for the cold or she was already taking care of it herself.

It was cold on December 22, 1978, in the town of Shakhty, a place as unadorned as its name, which in Russian means "the mines." Black mountains of coal slag rose from the flat yellow fields of sunflowers around the city. And there was a neat pile of coal in front of all the closely packed homes—single-story, with brightly painted walls and shutters but still somehow closed in on themselves—the sort preferred by peasants who move to the city. There were a few tall buildings of sooty brick in downtown Shakhty, whose central thoroughfare, Victory of the Revolution, had been bestowed with an immense statue of a victorious Red Army soldier brandishing a legendary Pepesha submachine gun.

Svetlana Gurenkova continued to observe the man in the beaver-lamb hat and the plump girl in the red coat. Now it was not only clear to Svetlana that the man was trying to talk the girl into something but that the girl herself seemed to be of two minds.

Svetlana still didn't like what she saw. Were they related? They didn't look like uncle and niece, more like strangers, neighbors at most.

The girl in the fur cap and red coat, Lena Zakotnova, was on her way home from school. It had been a regular school day with classes in a room where a portrait of Lenin watched over the children. There had been dancing classes which were fun. There had been time for giggling and secrets. She'd told her friend Olya that she might be getting some "imported" chewing gum from a nice old guy who sometimes got some. It wasn't every day that a pack of chewing gum made its way from Germany or France or, best of all, America to a gritty mining town in the south of Russia. But it had to be a secret or everybody'd want some.

After school she'd gone skating. As she had been gliding on the ice at the rink, Lena had heard her name called. It was her friend Natasha saying, Walk me home.

Lena stopped by Natasha's to use the bathroom. Then Natasha walked her up to the corner of Lenin Street where they said goodbye. A few minutes later a boy from Lena's school was sent to the drugstore by his father and, on the way, caught sight of Lena walking along Kirov Street in the direction of the trolley stop. She was alone.

But now she was no longer alone, she was talking with a tall man with glasses and a shopping bag in one hand. It was almost six, and darker. Svetlana kept unapologetically observing the man and the girl.

Then the man began to walk away and, after a moment or two, the little girl walked after him, so maybe there hadn't been all that much to it in the end. Either the girl's doubts had been dispelled or hadn't been serious enough when it came right down to making a choice. Still, Svetlana Gurenkova hadn't liked the look of it, start to finish.

But then her own streetcar came and she went home.

The man Lena Zakotnova had chosen to follow was Andrei Chikatilo, a dorm monitor at a local mining school, GPTU-33. Not only did he work with children, he had two of his own, a thirteen-year-old daughter and a son about the same age as Lena, who had celebrated her ninth birthday the month before. Chikatilo had also had a birthday recently. On October 16 he had turned forty-two.

Andrei Chikatilo had two residences in the town of Shakhty. He lived with his wife and children on 50 Years of the All-Union Leninist Communist Youth League Street. But he also had another house—a dilapidated three-room stucco shack with unusually low ceilings at 26 Border Lane of which no one knew but he. And he was on his way there now with the girl in the red coat beside him.

He had begun that day at home with his family, a steady, wage-earning husband, a father who never raised his voice to the children, a party member in good standing who read the newspapers and kept up with the world. A quiet man with the severely modest tastes befitting a true Soviet, he was content to wear the same brown and gray clothes year after year. The most any of his acquaintances might say of him was that he had a fondness for herring and played a pretty fair game of chess.

Chikatilo still retained a touch of his youthful good looks though there had always been something too sweet and weak about the lips—the face of a romantic idealist and Stalinist.

He had done everything right. Like all Soviet citizens he had served in the military, stringing cable and line for a KGB communications unit. Later, he had studied hard, earning three degrees—in the Russian language and literature, engineering, and Marxism-Leninism. He had thrown himself into party work, written article after article for the papers on Soviet patriotism and communist morality, and had even volunteered to work with the police as a "non-staff police assistant" and was issued the sort of flip-open red ID case that automatically commanded respect. He had done everything right, and everything still was wrong.

Just as it always had been. In his own version of his life, as secret as the house on Border Lane, Chikatilo had been born without eyes or genitals. Not literally, but close enough. As a child in school, he could never see what the teacher was writing on the blackboard. The blurred words streaked as his eyes moistened with rage and self-pity. And as a youth he was quickly to learn that he was incapable of erection, though not ejaculation. Later, upon very rare occasions with his wife, he was able to achieve sufficient erection to father children. But that never shook his belief that nature had castrated him at birth.

And fate had violated him even before birth. During the great Ukrainian famine of the early thirties, his older brother,

Stepan, was abducted and cannibalized. It was not a unique event for those times, but that didn't take the pain and horror out of it for Chikatilo's mother, who wept bitterly, copiously, every time she told him the story, which was often. And Stepan was the older brother who would have defended him against the world and people. But he had no one to defend him now, least of all himself, for Chikatilo always felt himself the most defenseless of men. He could not rise to an insult any more than he could to a woman.

All his life anyone could say anything to him and there was nothing he could do about it. The other children knew that about him right away, and called him every name. Over time his soul filled with tears and the piss of insults.

And the rough boys in the mining school where he now worked had seen through him fast enough. They smoked in front of him and just laughed when he told them to stop. He knew they called him "Goose" because of the way his sloped shoulders made his neck seem elongated, and because they thought him a fool, and didn't even bother to hide it. And now that word had gotten around the school that one of the students in the dorm had woken up to find his penis in Goose's mouth, they'd started calling him "faggot" to his face. Now when he came to a dorm room to enforce lights-out, the students would throw a blanket over him, beat him up, and kick him out. And just the other day some of the boys had come running up behind him in the park and knocked him to the ground, yelling vicious insults at him, a teacher, a grown man. This had so frightened him that he had even bought a knife and began carrying it with him at all times.

He had taken it with him on the morning of that day, December 22. The day before had been the anniversary of Joseph Stalin's birth, who would have been ninety-nine. And the night before had been the longest night of the year, the earth tipping its farthest from the sun. Perhaps it was that one extra minute of darkness that brought Chikatilo to equinox as well.

*   *   *

Now he and the girl, Lena Zakotnova, were almost to the secret house, just up the road and to the left. They were walking quickly because of the stinging cold in which even speech seemed a waste of energy. They'd be there in a minute.

It was the last chance he'd have to turn back: It only takes a second to break the spell, it only takes a few seconds to make up an excuse—to say he'd forgotten the keys.

But why should he break the spell, think up the excuse, speak the words, after everything that had been done to him? He would never have wanted to be born the sort of man who sniffs around the girls' toilet and peeks under the doors, he would never have wanted to be that sort of man, but that's the sort of man he was. He would rather have been a brave communist partisan fighting the enemy in the woods, taking prisoners and torturing them until they told the truth. He would have wanted to be a hero of exalted love, having even vowed in writing as a youth to touch no woman's genitals but his wife's. But he had found out that he was a man who hated to touch any woman's genitals though he could not keep his hands off his own, even fondling them through his pocket in the classroom, the boys hooting with scorn. He would have liked to have been the sort of man whose entry into a room would all by itself quiet those boys into full respect, the sort of respect boys are glad to give. The sort of respect they would never give him. Because he was a Goose, a faggot, and a fool.

He would have liked to have been the sort of man whose father returns from the war with medals on his chest and black boots gleaming, while everyone in the village cheers and throws flowers. But when his father returned home from a Nazi POW camp, they said he was a traitor for letting himself be captured. Only ten years of cutting timber in Siberia could expunge a sin like that. And so the village had not hurled flowers but insults at his father for having committed the crime of staying alive.

If Stalin said it was a crime, it was a crime. It would have taken a person much stronger than Andrei Chikatilo to resist the temptation to believe that Stalin was right, life could be a crime, his father could be a criminal—Stalin was above all fathers, he was the Father of the Country. And when Stalin died in 1953 Andrei Chikatilo wept, for he had lost a last protector. And he had so wanted to go to Moscow for the funeral, to offer his respects, but there hadn't been any money, there was never any money.

He would have liked to have been the sort of man to whose opinion his fellow teachers listened with quiet esteem. But to them he had only been the teacher who had gotten caught slipping his hands into little girls' pants. When instructions for staff reduction came, they had cut Chikatilo right away. And that had meant that he and his family had nowhere to live, for their apartment belonged to the school. And the best he had been able to find was a position at a grubby mining school in Shakhty, where they gave him an apartment that looked as though it had been through the war and didn't even have indoor plumbing. The look on his poor wife's face when she saw it for the first time . . .

And he shouldn't even be teaching in schools like that. He should have been a distinguished lawyer or a judge and would have been if they had only let him into the law school at Moscow State University. He'd done very well on the tests but, as he was told later on, a young man whose father Stalin had sent to Siberia could not be trusted with the grave responsibilities of upholding Soviet law.

His true vocation had been ripped from him like his eyes and genitals. Like his brother had been ripped apart. Chikatilo knew what they did, he'd seen the bodies of people who had starved to death in the famine that came right after the war, their still-meaty calves and buttocks carved away, his mother always telling him to hide or he'd be next.

After everything that had been done to him, shouldn't there

be one place on earth where he could do whatever he wanted?

There was such a place, the secret house at 26 Border Lane, whose threshold Chikatilo now crossed with Lena Zakotnova, flicking the light on, then locking the door.

When he shoved her to the floor, she was so stunned she did not even cry out.

This girl was going to have to obey all the rules of the secret house. She was going to let him unbutton her red coat and pull down her pants. Although he loved the sound of her screaming, she couldn't be allowed to cause any commotion that might get him in trouble, trouble was the last thing he wanted. What he wanted was silence and obedience.

He knew how to stop the screaming. Place his left forearm across her throat and press down with all his two hundred pounds. Her eyes begged a last mercy, then went blank. But her eyes had not closed. He pulled off her thick woolen scarf with a dark herringbone pattern and blindfolded her.

Now she was perfect, silent, obedient, alive.

But even when he had settled himself between the girl's cool, plump thighs nothing happened. Even moving in rhythm with her spasms brought him excitement, not erection. But now that no longer mattered. That was the sex of this place. And for one bright second he knew his most secret wish had been granted.

But then Chikatilo was amazed. He had thought he had taken his pleasure, but only because he did not yet know what his pleasure was. When his fingers were placing the sperm where it belonged, he was seized by a sudden desire to do injury to the girl's genitals; now the quality of his second orgasm was so clearly superior to the first that he could not mistake the meaning of this new knowledge, this new secret told in enactment.

The girl was still wheezing and thrashing. He looked down on her, having to decide. But if the girl told, his wife would never forgive him. Three jabs of his knife formed a triangle on her stomach, apex to the right. Now there was a new sort of stillness in the house at 26 Border Lane.

Perhaps it was because he had the girl under one arm like a small rug and was holding her school case in his other hand that Chikatilo forgot to turn off the light. Or he may have been too intent on discerning any figures moving along the unlit street of ramshackle houses. And once he was convinced there were none, he moved too quickly even to notice her blood spattering accusation outside his own doorstep. All that mattered was crossing the lot overgrown with cattails and weeds that led to the Grushevka River.

The only thing he could do now was throw her into the river, then hurl her school case in after her.

Even as he turned and strode away, the chill waters of the river were bearing the girl swiftly downstream. She was still alive.

CHAPTER 2

As soon as his six-year-old stepson came running in shouting, "Daddy, they pulled a girl out of the river," Alexander Kravchenko felt his heart sink. If the girl had been murdered, the police would be coming for him soon, and if she had been raped and murdered, they'd be coming all the sooner. The first thing they'd do is check if there were any people already convicted of similar crimes in the area. They'd find out that he had been convicted in 1970 for raping and murdering a girl about his own age at the time, seventeen. They'd see that he'd been given the maximum sentence for a minor, ten years. The record would indicate that, after six years in a labor colony, he had been released on August 12, 1976, to perform labor useful to the national economy for the remainder of his sentence, which came to three years, eleven months, and four days. But maybe they wouldn't even have to check the records, maybe somebody would just remember—Kravchenko, he doesn't live three hundred yards from where the body was found.

His son wasn't the only one relaying the news, word of mouth always travels fast in Russia. There was already a crowd of hundreds on the bridge under which the body had been found at one o'clock on the afternoon of December 24. And hurrying police always draw crowds in their train.

People jostled, craned, yelled questions. Only a very few could see the police photographer crouching to get a good angle on the girl, one that showed both her scarf tied around her eyes and the stab wounds on her bared stomach. The photographs taken later in the morgue would be blunter, interested only in the wounds, not the way the head fell to the left or that the full lips were open as if asking for something.

Crossing the bridge over the Grushevka River at that very time was Svetlana Gurenkova, the woman who, two days before, had observed with uneasy interest an older man talking to a girl in a red coat. Svetlana pressed her way through the crowd and confirmed her worst suspicions. Later that day, she informed the police that she believed she could serve as a witness. Her name and address were taken.

The police came for Alexander Kravchenko on the evening of that same day. He knew that by law they could detain him for three days or arrest him for ten. In either case he would then be charged or released. What mattered were the exact questions they would ask him after the usual formalities:

"Name?"

"Alexander Kravchenko."

"Date of birth?"

"February 23, 1953."

"Place of birth?"

"Ukraine."

"Nationality?"

"Ukrainian."

"Education?"

"High school."

"Party membership?"

"Not a member."

Then came the questions that really mattered, to them and to him.

"Where were you on the evening of December 22?"

"I returned home from work a little after six. Six ten. My wife

Galina had a guest, Tatyana Gusakova. I turned on the TV and watched a little bit of the first quarter of a hockey match. But the women don't like hockey and asked me to turn it off, which I did. Then the three of us ate together and drank a couple of bottles of wine. We talked about what we were going to do for New Year's. Tatyana wanted my wife and me to spend it with her and her husband, but I said we'd probably be going to my wife's brother's. Around nine o'clock I walked Tanya to the trolley stop, then went right back home."

He was lucky, he had an alibi that could be confirmed not just by his wife but by another person as well. All they had to do was bring them in and question them independently and they'd see he was telling the truth.

For some reason it took the police the full three days that they could hold Kravchenko as a detainee to interview his wife Galina and their friend Tatyana Gusakova. They each told the same story—Kravchenko came home around six, was sober, watched a little TV, then all three of them had dinner together, drinking two bottles of wine. They talked about New Year's, jobs, money, then Kravchenko had walked Tatyana to the trolley stop. Tatyana remembered asking Kravchenko if his wife would be jealous. The stories matched. And so, when the three-day term expired on December 27, the police had no reason not to release Kravchenko.

At around that same time the police appeared at the home of Svetlana Gurenkova, taking up her offer to serve as a witness and inviting her to come to the October Precinct station to make an initial statement. It turned out that her visual memory was so uncommonly good that a police artist was called in to work with her. He sketched as she described the tall slope-shouldered man with the glasses and hat, trying to coordinate his lines to her words. Finally, he produced a version that won her approval.

A copy of that picture was brought to the principal of school GPTU-33. The principal, Andreev by name, immediately recognized the picture as that of one of his teachers, Andrei Chikatilo.

"Not a word about this to anyone," said the policeman before leaving.

It was also on December 27 that two policemen, working the general vicinity of the crime, came across some bloodstains in the street between 25 and 26 Border Lane, which faced each other. They brought samples of the blood back and did the necessary paperwork for having a test run at the lab.

The house at 26 Border Lane proved to have been recently acquired by Andrei Chikatilo for the sum of 1,500 rubles. He was called in for questioning. He came with his wife, who supported him when he stated that he had spent the entire evening at home. Chikatilo was allowed to leave. But he still remained a strong suspect. Wives lie. The blood pointed to his door. And the principal of the school where he worked had identified the composite sketch as Chikatilo. And Chikatilo's neighbors on Border Lane had come home from the movies around nine o'clock on the night of the murder and had noticed a light on at Number 26. They had both remarked how nice it was that their neighbor was lighting their way. That light had burned all through the night and was still on the next day.

It was decided that Chikatilo merited further questioning but not until his past had been looked into.

But there were some twenty other suspects, including the victim's grandfather, who had to be questioned and checked. It would take some time for the list of suspects to whittle itself down to two or three.

The New Year didn't start well for Alexander Kravchenko. On January 7 he argued with his wife so fiercely that he struck her in the face. But as soon as the blood began streaming from her nose, he walked her over to the sink and washed her face, not even noticing a few drops of blood spatter on his sweater. They hadn't been getting along. There were arguments about money. But he couldn't tell her the truth, that until he finished serving his time, he'd never have much in his pocket. But she didn't know about that and didn't need to.

At least the police weren't bothering him, not a word from them since he'd been released on December 27. They were, however, still interested in Andrei Chikatilo. His work record showed that he had been employed as a teacher in the nearby town of Novoshakhtinsk, where several child molestation complaints had been lodged against him, resulting in his eventual dismissal. Moreover, there had been recent reports in the town of Shakhty itself of a man matching Chikatilo's description who had been chased away several times from the girls' toilets of public schools. Chikatilo was brought in for further questioning.

Chikatilo admitted to the incidents of child molestation with the shame of a good citizen who once had a terrible problem, but one which now, thanks to a good wife and loving family, he had been able to overcome. He said that he always suffered from "sexual weakness" but that now, in his forties, those things had come to mean less to him.

But why believe him, it was the oldest truth in the world that if somebody does something once, he'll do it again. And the evidence was good—the witness, the lighted window, the blood.

Then, on the evening of January 23, Alexander Kravchenko committed an act of petty theft, a chancy business for a man still on parole. The theft had been committed at a neighbor's house. The police searched Kravchenko's house the next morning and found the stolen goods in the attic. Kravchenko was arrested at work at three o'clock on that same day, the 24th.

The police had not been around to see him since he had been released almost a month earlier. Now he had brought himself back into their view and their custody. The fact that a suspect in the Lena Zakotnova murder case had been arrested on another charge was of course promptly reported to the man in charge of the operation, Deputy Chief of Police Chernatsky, who was well aware that this murder which had outraged the town had to be solved swiftly.

He also knew that you had to look beneath the surface, past alibi, into character. Chikatilo might have been the quiet, creepy type that couldn't keep his hands out of little girls' pants, but Kravchenko was a convicted rapist and murderer. He had done this already. And it's a lot easier to cross that line a second time. The thrust of all police training was to search for analogous crimes in a suspect's past—there was no better clue in the world. And there was no better evidence than the suspect's own confession.

And if Kravchenko was the murderer, he would of course have an alibi—at home with his wife and their friend watching TV and having dinner. But if Kravchenko was the murderer that alibi would prove to be false. And the best way to test the truthfulness of an alibi was to subject it to pressure.

Deputy Chief Chernatsky came to a decision: all efforts were to focus on Kravchenko. The machine can work fast once the order is given. The very next day Kravchenko's sweater was sent to the lab for a test to be run on the bloodstains. And the word got around the department quickly—Kravchenko was the main suspect now, the goal to break down his alibi and obtain a confession. No orders were needed, people knew what to do.

Before Kravchenko was remanded from a holding cell to prison, arrangements were made to transfer another prisoner, a thug and drug addict by the name of Miroshnichenko, to cell 36, so that he would be there already when Kravchenko arrived. Miroshnichenko was on the police's active list of paid prison "enforcers" and had been assigned number 7. Now he was told what his duties were and how much he would receive for performing them successfully. He was always glad to pick up a few rubles and it never hurt to do the police favors, hand washes hand.

In the meantime the blood on Kravchenko's sweater proved to be the same type as the victim's. But he insisted on his innocence, claiming that the blood must have been from his wife whom he had struck in the face during an argument. Luck was against him—it turned out that his wife and the victim had the same blood type. And the semen found in the victim's body was the same type as Kravchenko's.

Even though his cellmate beat him mercilessly every day on his return from questioning, Kravchenko maintained his innocence with the fervor of the truly innocent or the truly guilty.

But a killer's alibi had to be false, and a false alibi could be broken. Now Kravchenko's wife Galina was detained as a suspect in the theft for which her husband was being held. He had already confessed to it, emphasizing that he had done it alone. But the police knew all about them, a pair of sneak thieves who robbed houses together, so what was the difference whether they'd done this one together or not? The police were ready to indict her and her husband for five robberies committed between December 1977 and January 23, 1979, the total value of the goods stolen amounting to exactly 1,358 rubles and 40 kopecks.

But when she admitted that they had in fact committed robberies together, Galina found to her surprise that the men interrogating her—not investigators from the attorney general's office as the law required, but police detectives—were not really interested in the thefts at all.

Now they informed her that her husband had committed a homicidal rape in 1970, which came as a shock to her. And even more shocking was their statement that she was also being held as an accomplice to the murder of Lena Zakotnova for which her husband was being charged and which they said had taken place in her home. The police took pains to impress her that being an accomplice to murder was a serious crime and carried a long sentence.

It was all clear. The man she lived with, the man who punched her in the face when he was angry, had lied to her about his past and never told her the main thing—that he had raped and killed a girl. Now that man was going to drag her into prison just as he had dragged her into theft. It was also clear she could avoid prison by giving the police what they wanted, which wasn't all that much either, just to say her husband came home later, and not sober but drunk. She didn't want to betray him, she loved him. But the other choice was years in prison and she had a child.

Once the suspect's wife had testified that her husband had come home not at 6 but at 7:30, not sober, but drunk, it was legally possible to detain the other witness, Tatyana Gusakova, on the charge of giving false testimony. Some people cannot bear jail even for an hour and she was one of them. She screamed and yelled and beat on the bars. They knew she'd break quickly.

Not only did Tatyana Gusakova change her testimony as to the time of Kravchenko's return and his sobriety, she now recollected some useful details about their conversation on the way to the trolley stop.

He had said to her: "Tanya, would you believe it if I told you that I had raped and killed a girl?"

"Stop that crazy talk," she replied.

"I was just kidding," said Kravchenko.

Now the law required that Kravchenko be given the chance to confront his accusers.

"Are you out of your mind?" he cried to his wife. But even in his presence neither she nor Tatyana Gusakova changed their stories. Kravchenko was then dragged away for his next beating by his cellmate. Now that his spirit had been crushed, it shouldn't be long before he confessed.

Though both witnesses had been held longer than allowed by law, they were released only after the confrontation with Kravchenko. In the weeks that followed, the police kept dropping by to make sure they'd undergone no change of heart or story.

On February 16, 1979, one week before his twenty-sixth birthday, Alexander Kravchenko confessed to the rape and murder of Lena Zakotnova. Of course, at such an emotional moment memories can become hazy and, in reminding him of some of the pertinent details, the police were only telling him what he already knew all too well.

He even added some embellishments of his own—that he had been drunk and fallen down and the girl had even come over to help him, they liked that sort of detail. He also admitted that he had vomited after killing her. As for the knife, he'd thrown it into the river. Perhaps even then he was counting on the river being dragged and no knife being found, for the one thing Alexander Kravchenko knew now was that he must prepare for his trial, the only place he'd have the chance to tell the truth and be believed. At least now the beatings would cease.

What he failed to realize was that the first confession is always given the most weight, the initial cry of the soul is the one to be trusted.

Deputy Chief Chernatsky was pleased with the results and, following standard procedure, ordered all other investigation terminated and all material not connected with Kravchenko removed from the active case file.

Svetlana Gurenkova had become actively involved with the police in the search for the murderer after she had given the testimony that formed the basis of the composite sketch. Like any citizen she was outraged by the crime; unlike the other citizens of Shakhty she might have been able to do something to prevent it if she had reported that man to the police that same evening instead of boarding her trolley and going home. She too was glad to learn that the murderer had been apprehended and asked if she should come in to identify him.

"If you're needed, you'll be called," she was told.

She wasn't needed, wasn't called. And Principal Andreev

who had identified the composite sketch as Andrei Chikatilo was no longer needed either. At the time Principal Andreev had been instructed not to say a word about it to anyone. He was surprised no one from the police came back to him, but not surprised enough to keep from doing what he had been told.

Now there was a lot of paperwork to be done. Kravchenko's cellmate Miroshnichenko signed a sworn deposition to the effect that he had never under any circumstances applied physical force to Alexander Kravchenko. Any objections on that count could be forestalled on record.

They had plenty to send the case to trial. The suspect's confession, the testimony of his wife and friend, the analogous crime, the matching blood, the semen. There was no reason now to put any time into identifying the one fingerprint on the lock of the murdered girl's school case. It might not even be Kravchenko's, could be anyone's, her grandfather's. In fact, all other physical evidence unrelated to Kravchenko could now be destroyed, no sense in having it clutter up the place. It turned out that the blood found across from suspect Andrei Chikatilo's door had never quite made its way to the lab, just as well, the state had been saved a few rubles.

I nspector Issa Kostoev's life was marked by crime from the very start, the crime done to his people, his family, him.

On February 23, 1944, by order of Joseph Stalin, an entire nation, the Ingush, was packed into cattle cars and sent eastward into exile. The official charge against them stated: ". . . many Ingush have committed treason, have gone over to the side of the Nazi occupier, and joined the ranks of the saboteurs and spies dispatched by the Germans behind the Red Army's front lines . . ." The Ingush lands had not been occupied and many Ingush had fought and died in defense of the Soviet Union. The emptiness of the charge only made the punishment all the more cruel.

Only a year and a half old at the time, Issa Kostoev was too young to recall that month of hunger, degradation, and death as the trains crept from the green plains of the North Caucasus to the arid steppes of Kazakhstan. But the older people remembered and told the stories again and again until they became a part of Issa's own memory.

Though the operation took a few days, it was February 23—Soviet Army Day, a holiday for everyone else—that was seared into Ingush memory. The NKVD, as the Soviet secret police was known at the time, was in charge of the "resettlement." Trucks filled the squares of small towns and villages.

People were given one hour to prepare. There were any number of good reasons to obey. This was wartime, this was a Soviet government order, and it was the secret police enforcing it.

Issa would be told again and again how those unfit for travel or those living too far in the mountains for convenient transport to the train station had been herded into buildings that were then set on fire and sprayed with machine gun bullets. But this was Russia, Soviet Russia but still Russia, and so that meant that even the night of violence would be illuminated, if only momentarily, by a sudden, startling flare of compassion. A Russian soldier came running after one of the trucks with a sewing machine in his hands.

Panting, he handed it over to its owner, a woman with a two-year-old girl in her arms.

"Hey, lady, better take it, you might need it."

She took it. And with that sewing machine she eked out a living in the wilds of Kazakhstan, saving the life of that two-year-old girl who would one day marry Issa Kostoev and add that story to all the others he had heard.

The story of the train ride begun that day in late February was told again and again. The keen shame felt by his compatriots, all Muslims, at having to relieve themselves in the presence of others, each cattle car being equipped with a single hole in the floor. The doors were sealed shut and opened only periodically so that corpses could be removed. Sometimes the guards simply heaved them out, sometimes people were allowed to attempt a trackside burial. But those not back on the train on time were simply shot by guards positioned on the roof of each car.

It was not desirable that everyone should die. On the contrary, there was a use for those who proved hardy enough to survive. There were fields to plant and gold mines to work in Kazakhstan, where labor was short. By accusing an entire nation of treason and by arresting that entire nation, Stalin had turned them into convicts. And there was no cheaper labor than convict labor in Stalin's Russia.

But why? That was the question Issa heard asked again and again in his childhood of exile. Some people said that Stalin was not really a Georgian because Georgians were merry and expansive to a fault, which could hardly be said of Joseph Stalin. By temperament he was more like an Ossetian—crude and aloof. His mother was said to be Ossetian. And hadn't the poet Mandelstam said of Stalin that "every killing is a treat/for the broad-chested Ossete" in the lines that would cost him his life? And hadn't the lands of the Ingush been given to the Ossetians? But why was Stalin becoming so generous all of a sudden? No, there was simply no telling what an insane criminal would do or why he would do it.

By nature Issa Kostoev was strong, pugnacious, curious, and observant. As he grew he demanded answers to everything from why his whole nation had been unjustly punished to the meaning of his own name. That last question was easier for his father to answer. He told Issa that in the green pasturelands of the high Caucasus mountains every clan built its own tower. Those towers were almost a hundred feet high and positioned throughout the valley so that all were visible to each other. Fires could be built on the tops of the towers to signal invasion as they had been since the time of Genghis Khan. The middle sections were designed for defense, and, in peacetime, people lived in the bottom. The Kostoevs had once belonged to another clan but had broken away and formed their own, building their own tower. In their language, Kostoev meant "those who had gone their own way." Issa was told that the Ingush had adopted the Russian practice of the patronymic, a middle name formed from the father's first name plus an ending that meant "son of." Issa's father's name was Muhamed and so Issa's patronymic was in its Russianized form Magamedovich. And his first name? It was how the Ingush said the name of the Christian savior, Jesus. Then he knew who he was—Jesus, son of Muhamed, of those who had gone their own way.

There was never enough food, only enough to survive, and sometimes not even that. People weakened, sickened, died. Often it was impossible to attend the funeral of a close relative; no "special resettlee" as they were called could travel farther than three kilometers from their place of residence without permission of the local commandant. The penalty for violating this law was twenty years' hard labor. Those harboring anyone past the three-kilometer limit received five years' imprisonment. But even those not attempting to flee were constantly under the threat of eight years of imprisonment for "shirking socially useful labor and leading a parasitical way of life," which meant whatever the commandant chose it to mean.

Though Issa was the fourth child of six, his boldness soon caught the eye of the older boys and older men, who always watched to see who was daring, who was fearful. The boys were not only watched but tested for their courage. There was a ritual for this as there was for much else in their lives. One boy would walk over to another, pull a hair from his own head, and hold it in front of the other boy's face. If that boy blew on the hair, it meant that he had accepted the challenge to a fistfight. There were only two rules: never refuse, never cry.

One day Issa was waiting naked as his mother washed his single set of clothes, which she had stitched together from the remnants of the overalls his father had worn while loading ore at the mines. One of the older boys from his village yelled into the house: "Send Issa out to fight."

"Leave the boy alone," called his mother tearfully. "I'm washing out his clothes, he's got nothing on."

"Send Issa out."

Issa's mother wrung out his clothes but his shirt and pants were still sopping when he stepped outside, not the kind of clothes you want to fight in. A boy from another village was waiting. He plucked a hair from his head and held it close to Issa's face. It doesn't matter that your wet clothes will impede

your arms and legs, it doesn't matter that your mother is crying, and what you yourself might want matters least of all.
There was only one choice, the same choice that was always
there—be branded a coward forever or fight and fight to win.

His mother had to let him go out and fight. You were
doomed in this land if you couldn't fight. And besides, how was
she going to stop Issa? At six he was hopping onto coal trains
with his older brother Osman and throwing off as much coal as
they could until the train had gathered so much speed that
they would have to go leaping forward through the air into the
seven-foot snowbanks that covered Kazakhstan in winter.
Then the boys would drag their booty home on a sled they'd
knocked together, toss the coal in the potbellied iron stove,
and be the heroes of the day. A night without coal in the root
cellar of an adobe hut can be very cold.

Issa's mother accepted the traditions of her people, what
else could keep a people's memory alive in that wilderness?
She accepted it when her husband Muhamed married for a
second time, converting the Russian woman, Maria, to Islam,
which was considered a virtue in heaven. All the Ingush accepted Maria when they were deported, for Maria could have
said: "I'm not one of them, I'm Russian" and she would not have
had to share the grief and danger. But what Maria said was: "If
they're going, I'm going with them."

Muhamed, Issa's father, was a man held in great esteem for
his ability to reconcile people who were at odds. Only
Muhamed could find the one point on which conflicting desires
could balance. Sometimes he would reinforce that point by
telling a tale about Nasrudin, hero of a thousand jokes in which
Islam whispered its wisdom for those with ears to hear.

Sometimes Muhamed quoted the Koran which he knew by
heart, and had to, for he could not read. Whatever his means,
his goal was always the same, to find the only justice there
could be for them there.

In 1949 the lightning of Stalin's ill will struck again. Another resettlement, short notice, trucks, trains. And this time they went from bad to worse. At least where they had been living they had the cellar of an adobe hut, but in the new place there was nothing except for the gold mines they would have to work and a few tents. People immediately built sod houses, then went to work making bricks for more solid, winter-resistant structures. The Ingush weren't afraid of work and here only work could save their lives.

But there wasn't enough time, enough food. In one month Issa lost two brothers, Osman, with whom he had stolen coal, and Israel, both weakened by hunger and ravaged by illness. And in that same month, Maria, his father's Russian wife, lost a daughter whom Issa thought of as his sister. It was the same in every family.

In their conversations, the men never blamed the Russians. They never blamed the Bolsheviks and the revolution which they had welcomed in 1917, because the communists had promised to return them the lands stolen by the Tsars and the Cossacks. They only blamed Stalin, to them a local boy and a kind they knew.

The men ate alone and were served by the young men, who consider this an honor, the only dishonor to serve badly. That was a lesson Issa had to be taught only once. He was leaning against the wall waiting for his father's next command or the opportunity to pour a guest's drink, when he heard his father order another of the young men to fetch a pillow. Issa thought one of the older guests must be uncomfortable.

When the boy returned with the pillow, Issa's father said: "Give it to Issa, it'll make leaning against the wall more comfortable for him."

At dinner the men spoke of Stalin often and always with hatred. But it was not only the men who spoke of Stalin, the women sang of him as they were out working the fields, certain that no Russian could understand their language and certain that none of their own people would ever inform.

Issa would hear their songs as he walked the four miles to school:

You have destroyed our homes,
and stolen our country away,
may you not rest long in the grave
where first you are lain.

Stalin's crimes were so great that he could only be cursed after death.

Those lines came singing back to Issa in 1961 when, under cover of night, Stalin's body was removed from beside Lenin in the mausoleum on Red Square where first he was lain.

Issa had started school in 1950 at the age of eight. He proved a great reader, an ability the older men put to good use. Any scrap of newspaper that strayed through that part of god-forsaken Kazakhstan would be thrust on Issa and he'd be told to read every line to see if there was anything about the Ingush being allowed to return home. But there was never a word.

Issa's father did not seem to understand how far it was from where they were in Kazakhstan to the lands the Ingush call Ingushetia.

He said to his father: "If they let us go home, how will we get there?"

"If they say you're allowed to go home now," replied Issa's father, "I'd wash, put on clean clothing, and then start walking home."

"Father, don't you know you could walk your whole life and never get there?"

"Even if it was only to die and be buried there, I'd spend the rest of my life walking."

Now Issa not only listened to what the men said about life and people, Stalin and Russia, but read the books that were closed to them, no more than black marks on white paper. He was quick at math, sometimes too quick, shouting out the answer before anyone else had a chance, even though the teacher kept telling him not to. But it was literature and history that gave him what he wanted most, some hint, some clue, some picture of the country he had been born in but could not remember. For the Russian writers of the nineteenth century the Caucasus had been like America's wild West, full of savages who had to be subjugated but whose valor could be admired nonetheless. If he found a place name in a poem by Lermontov or a short story by Tolstoy, Issa would run to his father and ask if it was near where they came from.

But the greatest of all his discoveries was Shamil, who had stood off the Tsar's armies for twenty years in the middle of the last century. So his people had their own heroes who were even written about in books, bearded men of the mountains who refused to hide, run, or surrender but who fought all the fiercer for knowing they could never win.

All Issa had ever seen was his people in subjugation. Any guard could call you a "blackass," any guard could lash your mother from horseback for gleaning grain that would otherwise rot but was still forbidden them. And there was nothing you could do about it, no one to whom you could appeal.

But there could be some sort of justice in this world, as Issa saw on March 5, 1953, when the Father of Nations, the Greatest Genius of All Time, Joseph Stalin, died.

The teachers lined up the children in the corridor of the barracks that served them as a school. Tears in their eyes, they informed the children: "Our teacher, our leader, has died."

None of the Ingush children cried, except a boy named Satarov who was standing beside Issa and who burst into tears.

Then classes were cancelled for the rest of the day and the children dismissed. As soon as they were outside in the snow, Issa walked up to Satarov and said: "Why did you cry about Stalin dying?"

Then, forgoing the ritual of the plucked hair, Issa attacked the boy who had committed treason to his people with his tears. They hadn't been rolling around in the snow for very long when, as bad luck would have it, Commandant Kurbansky came by. Every child knew him, and he knew every child.

"You're coming with me," said the commandant to the two boys and led them off toward headquarters. On the way Issa whispered to the other boy: "Tell him we were just fighting, no special reason." But all the fool did was start crying again.

When they were almost to headquarters, the commandant ran into a man and woman he knew and stopped for a chat, sending the two boys to wait for him by a doorway. When Issa reached that doorway, he turned to see the commandant engaged in conversation and kept right on going, increasing his pace to a run.

It was nighttime before Issa had worked up enough courage to go home. He found a house full of weeping people, his mother, his brother, the neighbors.

"What's the matter?" he asked.

"They took your father."

Instead of telling them what he had done, he asked: "Who took him?"

"A policeman came and took him."

No one knew where or for what.

Finally, late that night, Muhamed came home.

"Muhamed, what happened?" asked everyone at once.

"Where's Issa?" was his reply.

Issa came into the room.

"Well, Issa, have you helped your family today? Oh yes, you've been a great help to us. What did you think—Stalin would come back to life if you didn't punch the boy?"

Perhaps uncertain of what a future without Stalin might mean for them, the police only imposed a fine of 100 rubles, a symbolic but serious sum. A collection had to be taken up. The sum was gathered, the police paid, a paper stamped and signed.

Issa was shamed, but not utterly, for any Ingush man would

rather be the father of the son who had fought than of the son who had wept.

Many Soviets had wept at Stalin's death, a few had rejoiced. Soon enough, though, they were all united by a fear of the future, for there is only one thing more terrible than a Russia ruled by a tyrant and that is a Russia ruled by no one at all.

Those who had been brave enough to hope when Stalin died soon proved the realists, at least for the short run. Beria, the unctuous rapist in pince-nez who had been head of the secret police, was arrested and rumored to have been executed by the man who'd replaced him. The three-man team running the country was soon dominated by the bald and bumptious Khrushchev who, though long known as one of Stalin's bully boys, still had a gusto, a taste for life, that set him apart from the bloodless apparatchiks.

Word got around that people were being released from the gulags by the thousands, even the papers seemed printed with a freer ink. By 1956 Khrushchev was denouncing Stalin at a secret party meeting, but word of that got around too. Everything was a secret and nothing was. In that same year the first shock of the new freedom reached Issa and his family in Kazakhstan. The three-kilometer restriction was lifted. The Ingush could now travel freely within Kazakhstan but were not allowed to travel outside it.

By then Issa was fourteen and old enough to earn a little money, loading or unloading trains, kneading clay with his bare feet. But he still found time for reading and studying. He had understood that a good knowledge of Russian was essential for anyone wishing to make his way in Soviet society. The older men still pestered him to read the newspaper cover to cover to see if there was anything written about their being allowed to go home. But for a year there was only silence on the subject. Then in 1957 the official announcement was finally made: Their country was to be united with that of the neighboring Chechens and reinstated as the Chechen-Ingush Autonomous

Province. Part of the Russian republic, it would still have some control over local matters, the dignity of a minimal sovereignty.

Some of the Ingush exhumed the bones of loved ones from the soil of exile to bury in home ground, others just simply raced back to the Caucasus. By 1958, when Issa's father had brought the family to the Kazakh city of Tselinograd en route home, a halt had been put to the flow of Ingush. Too many had returned all at once, there was a housing shortage, especially since some of the Ossetians who had taken over Ingush homes had come to think of them as their own.

It was painful and ironic to be halted on the way home, but there was nothing that could be done about it. Issa's father was still in his prime and now did not doubt that he would see the Caucasus again. And at least they were living like human beings in a city, an apartment, not a vegetable cellar or a sod house. And they were alive, they had survived, most of them.

Issa continued his education in Tselinograd, doing well in all his subjects. Under Stalin, higher education was closed to special resettlees, but that had changed now and it was not only possible, but necessary, to plan for his future.

He knew exactly what he wanted to be—a test pilot, breaking the sound barrier, his MIG hurtling with the speed of freedom across the blue, absolutely nothing could be grander.

But then when he was in the tenth grade and at the fateful age of seventeen, he got the chance to earn a little money acting as an interpreter for the local court. A few Ingush had been arrested for stealing from railroad containers. They only spoke their own language. Someone who knew both Ingush and Russian was required.

As Issa translated the questions posed by the prosecutor, the lawyer, and the judge, he found himself both oddly detached and excited as he thought: "That's not the way I'd have asked that question. You could come at it from a whole different angle."

It was fascinating, tempting. But not quite enough to divert him from his goal—the Kuybyshev Aviation Institute to which he traveled in the summer of 1960 to take the entrance exams. Kuybyshev was located a few hundred miles southeast of Moscow near a bend in the Volga. During the Second World War most of the Soviet government had been transferred to that city, even Lenin's mummy evacuated there for safekeeping.

Young men came from all over the country to compete and it was only natural that the combination of high spirits and rivalry should lead to clashes. Issa would have probably refrained if someone had not called him a "blackass," an insult that ran deep with the memory of injustice. The brawl which ensued was large enough to attract the attention of the police. Applicants who had taken part in the melee were refused entry to the Institute.

Heartbroken that he would never be a test pilot, Issa decided to study law, a good second best. Maybe someday he'd get the chance to be the one asking the questions.

Fool that he was, Chikatilo was no fool and knew what anyone in his position would know. Murder gave you three choices. Go back, stay where you are, go on ahead.

To go back meant to be amidst humankind again, the monstrous loneliness at last over. But it is not only a person's nature, but his acts that isolate him. Crime creates secrets and secrets create an isolation that can be broken only by a single force, confession. That Chikatilo knew perfectly well from his favorite novel, *Crime and Punishment*, where Dostoevsky resurrects his hero by having him reveal his killings to Sonya, the pure-hearted whore.

But to whom could he confess? Chikatilo had no friends, and that left only his wife and the police. But his pure, good wife must never know, he couldn't do that to her.

The second choice was to stay where he was, to swear—never again, a vow that must be carried to the very end to have any meaning. He could be like the man in the story he had read as a child and never forgotten. A beautiful worldly woman pulled up in her sleigh in front of a hermit's hut. Seeing that he was a deeply devout man, the worldly woman tried to seduce him by removing all her clothes. The hermit was so tempted by the sight of her beautiful naked flesh that he ran and grabbed his axe and cut off his finger. When the woman saw the blood, she screamed and ran away.

But he was no monk, and he'd made too many oaths already.

There was always the third choice, to go on.

Chikatilo was in no hurry to choose, the shock of being a suspect still not having worn off.

He went to work, came home, read the papers, watched television. Brezhnev wasn't looking good lately, and his speech was slurred.

The days grew shorter and colder until it was winter at last. The one hundredth anniversary of Joseph Stalin's birth passed on December 21, followed by the first anniversary of that night in the secret house.

Suddenly, on December 24, 1979, Soviet troops invaded Afghanistan and the electricity of war surged through Soviet society. On January 22, the physicist Andrei Sakharov, en route to a seminar, was detained by the police and immediately exiled, without even a semblance of judicial process, to the closed city of Gorky for having, nearly alone in a nation of 270,000,000, protested the invasion of Afghanistan. At the time of his arrest Sakharov was carrying a glass bottle in the hope that sour cream might be available at the university canteen.

The newspapers made it quite clear what the proper attitude toward Sakharov should be: a naive scientist meddling in things he knew nothing about, led astray by his Jew wife, Elena Bonner. He should consider himself lucky to be treated so humanely. People who break ranks when the country is at war deserve harsher punishment than a comfortable apartment in a well-supplied city like Gorky.

It wasn't only Afghanistan. Brezhnev had declared China the great threat to world peace, meaning it was the enemy of the Soviet Union. Hadn't Iran on the country's southern flank been taken over by Khomeni and Islamic fanatics? There were

NATO missiles in Turkey. That was one continuous stretch, Turkey, Iran, Afghanistan.

And the West wasn't losing any time in using the war as a pretext for attempting to humiliate the Soviet Union. As a protest against the Soviet presence in Afghanistan, America, West Germany, and Japan would boycott the 1980 Olympics in Moscow, tainting them, spoiling them.

In that same golden July of the poisoned Olympics, newspapers brought Andrei Chikatilo more than information, they brought him delight and danger. Everyone in the neighborhood knew what an inveterate consumer of newsprint the teacher Chikatilo was and that he could not bear even to part with a single issue, newspapers stacked everywhere in that rundown apartment on a street which bore the grandiose name of 50 Years of the All-Union Leninist Communist Youth League.

One summer afternoon three young girls, two of them six, one thirteen, came knocking at the teacher's door in the hope of his sparing them a few newspapers to help start the bonfire they wanted to build that night.

Their arrival was unexpected and caught him off guard. Suddenly he felt helpless before their young beauty, their slender, tanned arms and legs, their summer dresses, their little bathing suits. As soon as he had let them in, he locked the door behind them. "You want newspapers? We'll find you newspapers," he said, picking up one after the other in his arms, slapping their behinds and slipping his hand into their underpants to squeeze and stroke the little they had between their legs. As always, nothing excited him more than their hopeless wrigglings and unhappy cries. "Don't worry," he kept saying, "it's nothing so terrible. We'll find you the newspapers."

The girls finally fled in shame and terror. He'd done it again. Now it was only a matter of time before the police would come. At the very least he would be disgraced in his wife's eyes, at the worst his involvement in the murder of Lena Zakotnova would have to be reexamined. And again there was nothing he could do but wait. Nothing but read the papers, turn the page.

August came. Polish workers led by an electrician named Walesa took over the Lenin Shipyard in Gdansk. The Polish government agreed to nearly all the workers' demands—Sunday mass would be broadcast on the radio, an independent trade union called Solidarity was allowed to be formed. But clearly this was a strategic retreat that would precede invasion of some kind.

Then it was December again, month of the longest night and Stalin's birth and the second anniversary of the death of Lena Zakotnova and of Chikatilo's not having murdered again.

Then the year was gone, its ember flaring one last time on New Year's Eve, a perfect reason for Russians to drink themselves into oblivion. But Andrei Chikatilo celebrated it much more modestly, as befits a man of proud Soviet plainness, a father whose daughter had turned fifteen that year and whose son had turned eleven, a husband who had celebrated a seventeenth wedding anniversary and had himself reached the solid age of forty-four.

The new year brought change and hope.

On March 2, 1981, Andrei Chikatilo ended his career as a pedagogue and assumed a new position, one that even had a sort of dignified ring to it, Senior Engineer, Head of Procurement, at the Rostovnerud factory in Shakhty. His new job meant that he and his wife Fenya would no longer be working in the same place. As long as he was near her, he was under her power, glad to submit to her care and contempt; as long as he was under her power, he could be under no other. But now he would be on his own.

Now he would join the supply side of the Soviet industrial system which would require that he do a fair amount of traveling. He would have to go from one factory to another to see what he could scrounge up—talk, drink tea, swap, make deals—and then he would have to go back to pick up the goods because nobody delivered.

When he worked at school GPTU-33 and lived nearby on 50 Years of the All-Union Leninist Communist Youth League Street, his life was very circumscribed, he barely used his car. Now he had not only been linked with the industrial system but with the transport system as well, trucks and trains were what made the Soviet Union move.

What he saw at train and bus stations revolted him. Vagrants, sluts, beggars, drunks. They never worked a day and yet had money for shish kebab and vodka. He watched them go off laughing into the bushes, making no secret of what they were doing. And what galled him more than anything was the injustice—nature had granted the joy of life to the scum of the earth and denied it to him.

But he liked the new job because his colleagues were treating him well. Some of them were, however, a bit put off by his drabness. He was always neatly dressed but he favored grays and gray-browns. Not the sociable type, though once in a while he could be very talkative, glad to discuss world affairs, on which he was always up to date and had definite opinions. Still, there was a silence and a colorlessness about him that people in the end found either a little eerie or simply boring.

The coming of the good weather meant more trips to Rostov for supplies. He would travel alone by train to make the arrangements, then return with a driver, usually Gukov, to pick up the goods. Gukov would be surprised at how often Chikatilo preferred to remain in Rostov after they'd picked up the goods, but that was the Senior Engineer's business, he was just the driver.

Still, as an experienced driver, Gukov knew that wasn't the right way to do things. The right way was for the engineer from procurement to return with the driver and sign off for the shipment. That way, if there was any discrepancy between what they'd signed for at the pickup and what was delivered, there'd be someone with authority to deal with it. Sooner or later that way of doing things was going to cause problems.

But how could you blame a man for wanting to spend some time in Rostov? Who wouldn't want to walk down Engels, the main street of Rostov, on a nice day in early September? After the kilnlike heat of August the city would have begun cooling, the hot winds the locals thought blew in from Afghanistan at last dying down. Still, every so often breezes would raise clouds of the ocher dust that seemed everywhere in the town, only waiting for the wind to lift it into the light.

It was always pleasant to stroll down Engels past the university, where straight-backed blonde Don Cossack beauties mingled with black Africans with scarified faces. The Africans had to know Russian to study and would speak Russian with each other if they happened to be of different tribes or nations. Some of the locals didn't like the blacks. Didn't like their color. Didn't like their having stipends when Russian kids had to scrape by. Didn't like seeing them with Russian women, able to take them places with state money.

The university's main building was white and low, modern and nice-looking from a distance; up close the steps had large jagged pieces missing, the windows' grime speckled with ocher dust.

There would be plenty for a solitary man strolling Engels Street to see—remnants of the original fortress wall, an arrangement of cannons and cannonballs attracting young boys, a solemn plaque explaining that Rostov had been founded in 1749, part of Russia's drive against the Caucasus and Turkey, a drive spearheaded by Don Cossacks who made these lands their own.

A solitary stroller would see laughing schoolgirls with white bows licking vanilla ice creams on a stick as they skipped down uneven sidewalks whose hollows inevitably held puddles. And then of course there was the Intourist Hotel, a fourteen-story cement box whose facade seemed somehow to have rusted. Unsavory types always hung around that hotel, looking for foreigners, easy to spot, with their good shoes and good teeth and good haircuts, and then trying to buy dollars from them. Some of the teenagers would even steal icons from their grandmothers to swap for jeans.

Right after the hotel, a stroller could either continue along the sidewalk or enter a small park with benches whose deeply curved bottoms indicated that the manufacturer had a clear sense of who might be using them. Couples strolled or sat on the edges of the concrete pools, which held only stagnant water and cigarette butts and attracted bugs. In the very center of that little park is a monument to Sergei Kirov, its copper oxidized gray-green. In boots, jodhpurs, and military tunic, Kirov has one hand raised in greeting and salute. His hearty gesture was mirrored by his own words, which had a touch of rough Russian the locals would like and were inscribed at the base:

. . . WE'VE REALLY HAD COLOSSAL SUCCESS. DAMN IT, TO PUT IT STRAIGHT, IT JUST MAKES YOU WANT TO GO ON LIVING AND LIVING . . .

The words had been spoken by Kirov but carefully chosen by the person or persons who decided precisely which words would be carved, punctuation and all, into the light brown marble slab. The message was quite clear—Kirov was a good communist, the head of the Leningrad party, and a regular Russian guy who had just wanted to live. And what had happened? The Trotskyists assassinated him and Stalin had to purge the whole land of enemies. There were always some who whispered that it was Stalin who had had Kirov murdered because he considered him a rival and also because Kirov's murder gave Stalin the right to slaughter anyone he felt he needed to. But there were always whispers, rumors, jokes that shouldn't be told. Or even heard.

If the stroller glanced to his left as he passed the park he would have noticed a mass of cranes by what would soon be Rostov's Musical Comedy Theater. The city was on the move and everyone said it wouldn't be long before Rostov would be a "millionaire," which is what the locals called a city whose population had passed the million mark and was thus, in principle at least, eligible for extra benefits, possibly even including that most useful and prestigious acquisition, a subway of its own.

Past the cranes was the top of the three-story courthouse: made of the yellow brick with white classical trim often favored on official buildings in Russia, it had a proper mixture of the solid and the graceful. Rostov had been famous as a city of flamboyant crime since the days of the Civil War, when the defeated fleeing Whites made easy prey. Since then travelers to that city were always warned—watch out, they'll steal anything, they ride on top of a train and break the window and reach in and steal your suitcase. City of thieves and gangs, the locals even taking a perverse pride in crime's color and drama.

Not all of the crime was homegrown. Rostov is the gateway from the Caucasus into Russia and all sorts of eastern types could be seen on the sidewalks—simple country men in brown suits and worn argyle sweaters preferring to squat while waiting, laughing mustached Georgians in clothes too good to have been bought by honest labor. And Armenians had been there since anyone could remember and, of course, Jews, though the Nazis had slaughtered many during the war.

The dwellings were a mix of gray Soviet boxes and painted cottages that looked as if they had strayed into town from some village. Downtown was lush with great ornamented bastions, pastel-green and white, cranberry-red and white, the legacy of the last century when Rostov had prospered as a manufacturing and shipping town. The smell of fresh bread from open bakery doors mixed with the aroma of Russian cigarettes, black as the tobacco.

In the very heart of the city was the park of flower beds and trees in front of the House of the Soviets, the political center of Rostov province, of which the city of Rostov on the Don was the capital. This was the former site of a Russian Orthodox church that had been dynamited to make way for the future. But the past, at least the communist past, had been memorialized in an equestrian monument to the Red cavalry which had liberated the city from the tsarist Whites. The horse was huge and so heroically endowed that the locals often used it as a meeting place, saying, "See you at six, right under the balls."

There was much to see and smell and hear in Rostov on the third day of September 1981, but that would not keep a devoted reader from availing himself of the excellent newspaper section of the Central Branch of the Municipal Library. The library had all Chikatilo's favorite newspapers—*The Hammer, Evening Rostov, Young Communist,* and *The Literary Gazette.* Even though he was no longer a teacher of Russian literature, that didn't mean that he wouldn't try to keep up. Factory work was beneath him, as his wife was forever reminding him.

There was much to read about, a year had passed, the insolent Poles still not having been taught a lesson. But then it was already after five and time to get going. Chikatilo could either catch a train home to Shakhty or spend the evening in Rostov at the factory's apartment on Petrovsky Street. It was still light when he came out of the library and headed for the heart of Rostov, the intersection of Engels and Voroshilov, thick with people and buses at that hour.

What initially caught Chikatilo's eye in that evening light, those evening crowds, was Larisa Tkachenko's bright claret-red jacket. She was a wild girl and she looked it. Having just turned seventeen in late June of that year, she was even more rebellious than she'd been in the past year, when she was forever in trouble for climbing out her dorm window to meet soldiers and spend the evening with them. She had arrived in Rostov that day, September 3, from the state farm on which her parents lived and worked. She'd gone there to pick up some warm clothing, September could be a fickle month. She'd arrived in Rostov somewhere around one-thirty in the afternoon, and was supposed to have then gone to her school, GPTU-58, located at 119 Engels, where buses would be waiting to take the students out to the Kirov State Farm to help with the harvest. Some students liked the open air, the camaraderie, the bon-fires, guitars and songs in the evening, but that was for young people who were still romantic about love, young people who hadn't been around like Larisa Tkachenko.

The man she saw approaching her was big and tall but didn't seem dangerous as some big men did. He was slope-shouldered, bashful looking, his large glasses and briefcase lending him a bit of an intellectual air, a teacher, maybe a bureaucrat, anyway someone who made his living with his mind, not his hands.

He was easy to talk to, he asked the usual questions, and had the usual things in mind, a little fun on the other side of the Don where there were half-naked couples under every bush and you had to be careful not to disturb anyone.

They began crossing the bridge over the Don. The only passenger and vehicle bridge over the river, it is believed by Rostovians to connect Europe with Asia. Though geographers might disagree, it was plain to the people of Rostov that the endless steppe which began on the left side of the river was nothing if not the wilds of Asia. There was always too much traffic for the bridge, always too many trucks and cars breaking down; it looked like a city being both invaded and evacuated.

The Don was sallow with the effluents released by the great agricultural machine factory just up the river. But there were green islands in the middle and sleek white tourist ships glid-ing on the even stream along with barges. Anyone seeing an older man in glasses with a briefcase in hand walking across that bridge with a wild-looking young girl in a claret-red jacket would have known just where they were headed and just for what.

He knew he should be grateful to her, for being so light and easy about it, for being willing to give pleasure to a man of his age when she could be out cavorting with one of the lusty young sailors or soldiers who filled the town, pants tucked in their boots, their hats cocked rakishly. It was still summer and half of Rostov was on the other side of the river, drinking and eating, laughing and fucking. Why shouldn't he be there along with them? Why should he be denied the normal pleasures of life? This wild young girl named Larisa in the claret-red jacket might just restore him to health, why not?

When they had crossed the bridge and were, by local reckoning, in Asia, they turned to the left on the asphalt path that led past the settlement of closely packed summer cottages, rewards for good workers. The acacias, as typical of Rostov as birches are of northern Russia, made huge corridors of cool shade. They walked for a little less than half a mile down the asphalt path that ran by cafes and restaurants where people feasted on shish kebab, plump tomatoes, black bread, and vodka, then turned onto a dirt path that led into a dense stretch of forest where they could be alone. They had to put some distance between themselves and others, those already there and those who might be coming later on.

Maybe this time it would be beautiful, as beautiful as in the books he'd read and the movies he'd seen as a youth. At least maybe this time it would be easy and natural and normal, and if he needed a little help like the kind his wife sometimes gave him, that sort of girl would probably be willing to lend a hand. Maybe this time he would want what everybody wanted, and do what everybody could do.

The vast arched steppe sky was becoming a deeper and more royal blue. The city still glowed with the last of the day's heat and electric light as the first stars emerged. There was a clean smell from the river and the faint aroma of sun-warmed earth. They were well in the woods now, just a little farther and they'd be far enough away.

When they had reached a spot magic with privacy and solitude, Andrei Chikatilo threw Larisa to the ground and tore her clothes from her until she was naked. Rough, but still in bounds.

Chikatilo had crossed the Don with Larisa in the keen hope that he could be like everyone else, every monster's dream. But he was not, and to be made mindful of it again by his flaccidity and her mockery of it was more than he could be expected to bear. But he also remembered what he had learned almost three years before in the secret house, his pleasure was not in the fondling of genitals but in their injury.

Larisa fought hard, but Chikatilo's hands were connected by a band of muscle that ran in a horseshoe-magnet shape across his back and shoulders and he squeezed the consciousness out of her in a minute. Now he was so angry he punched her face and packed her mouth with dirt.

Chikatilo lay himself back down on her. Now his rage was in his teeth and he began biting her neck and arms, each incision harder as he drove himself to frenzy. Then the fury was upon him, having consumed the past it was ready to create a new present and new future. Taking her breast between his teeth, he yanked his head back, ripped off her nipple, and swallowed it, becoming for the first time, in a single instant, what he truly was, a cannibal.

Now some mixture of innate tidiness and the desire to appear normal caused Andrei Chikatilo to put the sperm where it would have gone had he been capable of penetration. Taking a short, hard twig, he nudged the sperm to where it belonged, then did her so much vaginal injury that his hands were as red as his mouth.

Chikatilo rose, retrieved her clothing, and wiped the blood away on it. Briefcase in hand, he was about to leave but then, taking one last look, he decided she could not be left lying there naked, that wouldn't be right. Chikatilo knelt back down beside her, opened his briefcase, and then slowly covered her body with pages from the newspapers *Pravda* and *The Young Communist.*

C H A P T E R 5

Issa Kostoev quickly found that the law, not the sky, was his element.

He devoured it all—Aristotle, Roman law, civil law, family law, criminal law, the A's he received more a by-product of his passion than a goal in themselves, though every victory always counts. But those were hard years, education may have been free but life was not. Although his father suggested that Issa audit lectures and take the final exams rather than enroll as a full-time student, Issa would hear none of it. He wanted the real thing and he was willing to support himself, unloading freight cars if need be.

It had been a hard choice to remain for another five years in the land of exile, in Kazakhstan. The capital city, Alma-Ata, where the university law school was located, did have its beauty. Only a few hundred miles from China, it rested on a high plateau in the foothills of the Pamir Mountains, exquisitely white and finely silhouetted against a deep blue sky. The streets of the city were strewn with mossy boulders from the frequent avalanches. During the war, many of Russia's leading artistic lights like the film director Eisenstein had been evacuated to Alma-Ata, which had over time become Sovietized. But it was still a city of the East where bards recited sagas from memory, accompanying themselves on an instrument that was supposed to be a direct descendant of the ancient Greek zither. Old men with silvery beards and blue turbans still sat in the teahouses discussing the Koran and Sufi brotherhoods.

There had been practical reasons for studying at the law school of Alma-Ata University. It was considered third best in the country and Kostoev had no chance of getting into either Moscow or Leningrad. Chikatilo had been told that he had failed to gain entrance to Moscow State University Law School because his father had served time under Stalin. It didn't matter that his father had been punished for returning from captivity alive, the black mark was on his record. And Kostoev, as a former "special resettlee," had no chance either.

But remaining in the land of exile, though practical, also had the effect of keeping the wound open. Kazakhstan would forever be the place to which his family and his people had been banished though they were innocent of the charges of treasonous collaboration, as innocent as he, a two-year-old, had been. Kazakhstan would forever be the place he had been where two brothers and a sister had died, where he had seen his mother cringe under the whip, and where the penalty for stealing was a year for every kilogram. In some way it was only fitting that he studied law in that place of injustice.

It was a five-year program, time enough for certain things to come clear. He soon had the satisfaction, given to few, of knowing exactly what he wanted to do with his life—to become an inspector in criminal cases for the Attorney General's Office. What especially fascinated him was the art of interrogation. It raised profound questions. How do you establish psychological contact with a suspect and how do you maintain it? How do you win trust and destroy defenses? How do you get a man to do the one thing he does not want to do—confess to a crime which could cost him his freedom or his life?

Apart from course work, there were two additional requirements. Every degree candidate had to write what was called a "diploma paper," a long and serious analysis of some aspect of criminal law. By then Kostoev had understood that an investigator must have a deep knowledge of the variety of human types and of criminal personalities. Logic was the investigator's chief weapon, but it was useless without intuition, experience, and a healthy appetite for precisely that sort of one-on-one encounter.

But that was all school, theory, books. Issa Kostoev longed for the real thing, the action. Fortunately, the second requirement for graduation was practical work, a mix of on-the-job training and a way of filtering out the students who didn't have what it takes.

He could have gone home to Ingushetia, whose newly established province could use dynamic young men like him, but instead Issa insisted that he be sent to the city of Vladikavkaz, which was entirely in the control of the Ossetians who had stolen large stretches of Ingush land and refused to surrender them.

"Issa, you're crazy," said one friend. "They hate us there."

"I know," said Issa. "But I don't want to go to Ingushetia. Too many people know my father, too many people know me. I don't want relatives and friends coming around trying to influence me."

Again there were practical reasons. Vladikavkaz was close to home. He could visit his family and go up into the mountains with his friends and cook a lamb over an open fire by one of the torrential white streams that raced from the snows on the stony Caucasus through green mountain pastures to the fields below.

His friends were right, of course. They would hate him there in Vladikavkaz, he'd be walking into a lion's den. They'd hate him because he would remind them of their crime or, more precisely, that they were accessories to Stalin's crime of deporting the Ingush nation. The Ossetes had immediately taken Ingush cities, lands, homes, whereas the mountain Jews, themselves knowing the taste of exile, would have no part of it and the local Georgians had often been arrested for giving refuge to "enemies of the people." Issa Kostoev might not be able to test airplanes, but he could still test himself.

At first during his practical in Vladikavkaz he worked on the most minor of cases—shortchanging, hooliganism—and always under the supervision of a qualified investigator. Still, he got the chance to interrogate, to play that fateful game of question and answer, mind against mind. He also wrote up indictments, for which he proved to have a considerable flair. He knew which details were absolutely essential and could construct a logic that led the reader as firmly as a guard leads a prisoner to a cell. One of the prosecutors even praised Issa in front of the others, which won him a moment of glory and weeks of added enmity. More important than either was the fact that at the end of Issa's first month, the city's Attorney General, a Russian by the name of Dimitrov, had assigned him the first case he could run on his own.

A teenage girl had been detained for stealing jewelry from apartments while there under the pretext of registering children for school. She was now free pending further investigation. Kostoev summoned her for questioning, but she failed to answer the first summons and the second. Finally, the third time around, she deigned to appear. She was slovenly, insolent. Kostoev told her to wait.

He went to the Attorney General's Office and said: "We have strong evidence against her. I want her arrested."

The Attorney General agreed.

Kostoev returned and announced to her: "You are under arrest."

"What the hell do you mean? When I was in the holding cell, the chief of police came down and promised me if I fucked him, they'd let me go, just give me a little fine, that sort of thing. And here you are throwing me back in jail."

Kostoev wrote down everything she said, then had her taken off to a cell. Then he went back and reported to his protector, the municipal Attorney General, who in turn called the Attorney General's Office of Ossetia.

All hell broke loose. Who did this kid think he was! Him, a nobody, hasn't even graduated yet and he's taking on the chief of police, a Colonel? And a fucking Ingush to boot! The gall, the nerve, the balls.

But it was too late, the bombshell had exploded. A case would be brought against the chief of police for having illicit sexual relations with a minor while she was being held in detention. But Kostoev had caused enough trouble for a while and was taken off the case. No matter how it ended, there were many people who would never forget who'd started it.

After the four months' practical work in Vladikavkaz, Kostoev returned to Alma-Ata for the written and oral exams and to complete his diploma paper on the tactics of interrogation. No sooner was that done than Kostoev was embroiled in yet another row. He insisted that he be sent back to Vladikavkaz even though the rule was that inspectors should return to their native region and serve there. But, as the Russian saying goes: It's absolutely forbidden but, if you really want to, you can. He really wanted to.

An exception was found, an exception made. The Attorney General of Vladikavkaz wrote a special letter of request, and that carried sufficient weight. It was 1964 and Kostoev was on his way back to Vladikavkaz where they now hated him more than ever.

Now there would be no more poring over scholarly tomes but reading the literature he liked best—actual cases, the same drama of crime and criminal, victim and witnesses, over and over, yet each different, each a mystery. The pay, however, was miserable. It encouraged corruption by assuming it. For Kostoev the choice was stark and simple, either room or food, not both. He slept in an empty office and washed himself so vigorously with cold water in the morning that no one could tell that he hadn't just come from a good night's sleep at home in bed.

He often doubted the wisdom of his choice. There were too many obstacles, too much hostility. As he knew from reading about test pilots, every craft has its stress limit. But in every instance the doubts were overcome and Issa Kostoev remained in Vladikavkaz, a city whose Russian name means Master of the Caucasus.

If the law was his passion and interrogation his art, then murder was to become his specialty. It was the most serious crime and the most mysterious. Why, how do people cross that line? And, from the inspector's point of view, murder was also the most dangerous crime because, if injustice were done, an innocent person could be executed. The stakes were the highest.

Interrogation required that every sense be working at its peak. When questioning suspects or witnesses, you had to be attuned to the tones of truth and be able to detect the hollow ring of a lie. At the same time you had to be able to read faces, maintaining eye contact as long as the subject could bear it while still being alert to fleeting expressions at the corners of the lips. And the hands had a dialect of their own.

And there was another simple secret—unremitting work. There was no getting anywhere in his field without joining the party, too, though for too many colleagues that signaled something like a sinecure, semiretirement, a cushy post, a few hours in the office before a long, heavy, and vodka-laden lunch.

Hard work paid off. Inspectors were judged by how many cases they solved and his rate kept mounting. They had to promote him. There were still plenty of people who hated him, but not enough to stop him. Perhaps they had underestimated Kostoev's own hatred for injustice, especially that committed by the judicial system.

Promotions also meant increases in pay and now, after nearly a year and a half on the job, he no longer had to choose between food and lodging. He was in his mid-twenties, not too early at all to think about marrying and starting a family. At least, that was his father's adamant opinion.

"Issa, when are you going to get married? I can't start looking for brides for your younger brothers until you've got a wife," boomed his father. They weren't afraid of noise and emotion in that family.

When the row subsided, Issa had to acknowledge that his father was right. It was time.

It had to be an Ingush woman. But in all the years before he began working, he had met very few women, because Ingush custom kept them strictly apart, especially when they became old enough to interest young men. No dances, not even movies for them.

Yet there had been one woman, Asya. He hadn't seen her for six years but, he noticed, when the question arose she came right back to mind.

Their first encounter occurred when he was still a student at the Alma-Ata University Law School and had come home for vacation. It was also the Muslim holiday of Kuraza, a rare chance to be in public company with young Ingush women. A friend of Issa's suggested they visit a certain family whose daughter, Asya, was said to be beautiful. And indeed she was an Ingush beauty with fair skin and rich reddish-brown hair, her nose prominent and slightly hooked as the Ingush prefer, a touch of Asia in the shape of her eyes. Issa's friend made his choice on the spot and asked Issa to intercede for him in asking for her hand. A loyal friend, he complied.

But Asya would hear none of it. "I'm still at the university and I'm not about to marry anyone!" she replied fiercely.

So, it was the lovely, volatile Asya, determined to become an architect, who now came back to mind. A little sleuthing and Issa learned that Asya was still single and now working in an architectural firm in a nearby town. She had succeeded in attaining her goal. In that, she was like him, and not only in that. She had been born in the same year as Issa, 1942, and she had been deported in the cattle cars on the same day, the infamous 23rd of February, 1944. Her father had been a war hero, killed in an offensive against German paratroopers, but even that had not mitigated her fate in the slightest. She had known the bitterness of exile and the bittersweet taste of land and freedom only partially returned. The most important things could be spoken of between them but would never need to be.

Asya's friends thought it was a horrible idea. "Marry an investigator! They drink like fish and don't earn a kopeck!"

She paid them no attention. She knew she'd met her match. How could she resist a man brimming with such self-confidence that he could in all seriousness declare: "Asya, one day we'll live in Moscow and I will be a General!" Asya would marry him, even though that meant moving to Ossetia, to Vladikavkaz, to a place where her husband was feared, re-spected, hated, and, except for a few friends among the Os-setes, alone in the world.

Within a year they had their first child, a son, whom they named Timur after Tamerlane, the great conqueror who had swept out of Asia in the fourteenth century and whose remains now lay in a mosque of Islamic aqua in his legendary capital of Samarkand.

That was 1969. Issa had been with the Vladikavkaz Attorney General's Office for five years. He had come as a raw and rambunctious twenty-two-year-old and was now a married man, with a young son. But he was still rambunctious, as he was about to demonstrate again.

That year he was assigned to review the case of a woman who had been sentenced to death for murder, a conviction that had already been once upheld. The woman was on death row, and this would be the last review before her sentence was carried out.

Three or four investigators had already worked on the case.

There were depositions, reports, the court proceedings, the findings, fifteen volumes of evidence. Issa sat down to read.

An old woman had been murdered with a poker. It had been a long and painful death. There were more than a hundred wounds. Although many points were unclear, the court had accepted the following version:

The old woman lived alone and needed someone to look after her, do the shopping, clean the house. The old woman had some money and could pay. A fifty-year-old woman by the name of Gavrilova had taken on the job and done it so well that the old woman promised to will Gavrilova all her property upon her death.

Gavrilova lived elsewhere and had a job selling meat pies at the train station. Taking care of the old woman was becoming more of a burden all the time and so Gavrilova was glad to find a young student who was looking for a room. A deal was made. In exchange for room and board, the sixteen-year-old Natasha Kuznetsova, a student at the local railroad institute, would assume the care of the old woman.

One day, a neighbor looked in the old woman's window and saw her dead on the floor. The police were called and they broke down the door, having first determined that it had been locked from the outside. It was obvious that the killer had a key. It didn't take them long to learn that there were only two keys to the apartment, one of them in the possession of Natasha, the student who lived with the old woman, and a spare kept by Gavrilova.

Natasha was picked up at school and brought directly to the scene of the crime, which was a confusion of police, neighbors, photographers, experts.

Natasha's key was found in the apartment. The only other key was found later, in the possession of Gavrilova. The door had been locked from the outside. There were only two keys. The logic was hard and clear—the person with the other key had locked the door from the outside, and that person was the killer.

Under questioning, Natasha had broken and confessed. She said that one night, Gavrilova, greedy for the inheritance, had come to the old woman's house with a friend named Boris. They had killed the old woman with a poker and forced Kuznetsova to take part or be killed herself. They then forced her to leave the apartment with them, telling her to say that she hadn't spent the night there.

The student Natasha Kuznetsova was given five years as an accomplice. Gavrilova had protested her innocence all the way to death row where she now awaited her fate. Boris had never been found.

Reading certain depositions again and again, monitoring the evolution of a story into a confession and a case, Kostoev decided that he didn't like the smell of it.

But the logic of the keys was hard to refute. Still, there was a stronger logic, the one which he called the "logic of life itself." If Gavrilova wanted to murder the old woman, she'd have had plenty of chances in all those years when she was the only one taking care of her. Why did she need to involve the student, not to mention the elusive Boris? And why kill the old woman with a poker when it could have been done in a way that made her death look natural and not cause any suspicions about Gavrilova, the one person who stood to benefit?

He decided to visit Gavrilova on death row. She was in a small dark cell with only one small window at the very top of the wall.

Plump, dark-haired, Gavrilova was more than twice Kostoev's age and seemed to be a good and simple Russian woman but, if there was one thing he was learning, it was that all sorts of people commit murder.

"Son," said Gavrilova, "it's going on two years I've been in prison, almost four months here on death row. Do you think you could look into my case? I never killed anyone, I just can't prove it. It's just Natasha who says I did it. It's terrible here but I know they won't execute me."

"How do you know that?" asked Kostoev.

"One night Saint Michael came to me in a dream and said, 'Your life will be saved by a man who will prove that you are right.' "

"And what else did Saint Michael say?"

"He said that every day a dove would fly to the window of my cell to check that I was still alive. And there hasn't been a day that dove hasn't come to my window and sat and cooed a while before he flew away again."

Rechecking the student's testimony, Kostoev saw how it could be demonstrated to be a tissue of lies. There was sufficient doubt to release the woman from death row and to question the student further. The mere fact that her key had been found in the apartment no longer seemed so compelling, especially since the student had been brought directly from school into the confusions of the crime scene.

Enough reading had been done, it was time to do some writing of his own. He wrote up an order for Gavrilova's release and then went to the prison where she was held. He did not inform her at once, fearing that the shock might cause her a heart attack. Only gradually did he let her know that she would be released that day, that hour. Gavrilova was stunned, disbelieving.

So was the warden.

"Here's her release," said Kostoev. "Free the woman."

"What are you talking about!" objected the warden. "She's a convicted murderer."

"Comply with the release. It's been stamped. I wrote the release and I'll answer for it."

Not only did Kostoev obtain Gavrilova's release, he secured another order—that the student, Natasha Kuznetsova, up for early release, be held for another three months.

He was certain he was doing the right thing but that didn't

do much for his peace of mind, especially on that Sunday when a car was sent for him. He found the municipal Attorney General in the back seat. They had both been summoned to Moscow for a review of the case by a high-level panel.

"Do you see what you've gone and done now?" said the Attorney General.

Kostoev heard the question phrased another way in Moscow by a woman on the review panel.

"How could you possibly release her?"

"Read the case, you'll see."

Kostoev was given a hotel room and told to await further word from the panel, which would need several days to review the material. After four days of sitting in his room and preparing answers to any possible question, he could not bear the suspense another second and went to the building where the review board was meeting. He was told—"We're still reading, still looking into it."

Finally, a few days later, he was called in. The collegium, as the review panel was officially known, had assembled. Kostoev entered the room with both anxiety and the tremulousness of immense respect for people he considered "gods." The Attorney General was also present.

Several cases were to be reviewed that day but Kostoev's had been given first place. After the facts of the case had been stated, the woman who had asked him how he could have freed a murderer now rose and said: "Kostoev obtained Gavrilova's release and has requested that the student Natasha Kuznetsova be held another three months so that he can question her. Kostoev's decision was the right one and we owe him an immense debt of gratitude. We ourselves are at fault for having treated the case so superficially in the past . . ."

The Attorney General was hauled before the panel. The Russian Attorney General said: "Explain how this happened."

"I was on this case a long time," said the subordinate, the Ossetian Attorney General.

"Your behind was on the case. And it should have been on a chair while you sat down and read the files like Kostoev did."

"I'm sorry. Forgive me. I fought at the front, I've put twenty-seven years in the judicial system."

He was forgiven. In the corridor he walked over to Kostoev and said: "Thank you for what you did. I'm glad you were right, even though they made it hot for me. But we've still got some investigating to do."

Kostoev returned home from Moscow with a stuffed bear for his one-year-old son, Timur. Giving him the toy, Kostoev smiled and said: "Your daddy saved a person's life today."

Kostoev began questioning the student, Natasha Kuznetsova. Though his skills at interrogation were now well honed, the young woman proved resistant. But he unmasked one inconsistency after another in her testimony until finally she broke.

There had been no Boris. But there had been a boyfriend, hers, who had taken to spending the night with her. The old woman had objected. One day, during an argument, she had struck the old woman with the poker. The old woman fell to the floor, bleeding, unconscious, probably dying. The choice was simple, stark—either face punishment for what she'd already done or finish the job and cover her trail. But the girl was young and knew nothing of murder, which was why there had been more than a hundred wounds.

And the key? She had just slipped it into the apartment when the police had brought her there and the place was packed and confused. Couldn't have been easier.

Kuznetsova was sentenced to ten years, the maximum penalty for a minor.

Kostoev had taken a risk and it had paid off. It was a triumph but one with disturbing echoes. How many Gavrilovas were there in the country awaiting execution for murders they had never committed?

But he couldn't think about that constantly or it would

drive him mad. Sometimes he just had to forget everything and walk Peace Avenue, the main street of Vladikavkaz, enjoying the twilight, the sidewalks streaming with people. That's what he was doing one spring evening when a woman came out of nowhere to fall at his feet. She threw her arms around his legs and began kissing his feet. A crowd formed at once.

When the woman leaped up, Kostoev saw that it was Gavrilova. Tears in her eyes, she cried out: "Everyone, everyone listen! This man saved my life! I was on death row and he saved me . . ."

Every time he saw her coming after that, Kostoev crossed the street.

He did not want public adulation. Whispering his pride to his son was one thing, but this was quite another. He did his job because he loved his work and hated injustice inflicted by the very system responsible for administering it.

But corruption was hardly confined to the judicial system, as Kostoev learned when he was asked to look into the activities of a local factory that made apple wine. It was clear that millions of rubles were being embezzled, but no one could figure out exactly how.

Kostoev sat down with books on vinticulture. When he understood how wine was made, he was ready to look into how this particular factory was making it. Each year the factory's managers turned in receipts for 1,000 tons of apples and were reimbursed a million rubles. What he discovered was that they were buying only 100 tons of apples, substituting filler for the rest, and pocketing the remaining 900,000 rubles. The investigation lasted a year and a half; fifty people went to jail.

The murder case heard by the collegium had first brought Kostoev to the attention of Moscow, and the apple-wine investigation had won him additional renown. In 1974 he was transferred to Moscow to work in the Attorney General's Office, in what was officially known as the Department for Investigating Crimes of Special Importance.

In the years 1970–1972 Kostoev had achieved a 100 percent rate in solving murders. His colleagues in Vladikavkaz had pressured and entreated him: "Don't stick us with such a high standard. What'll we do if you're transferred?" There were very few people in Vladikavkaz who were sad to see Kostoev leave for Moscow, from where he would be twice assigned to the city of Rostov on the Don, once on a small matter of corruption, and once to track a murderer who killed with fists and hammers, knives and teeth.

PART II

CHAPTER 6

Chikatilo was free.

Whatever doubts had hounded him in the nearly three years between his first murder and his second were now dispelled. Those doubts, those questions, arose from the choices he confronted—to confess, to repent, or to continue. But Chikatilo had made his choice on a warm September night on the left bank of the Don where the screams of the dying girl could, from a distance, be mistaken for cries of love.

Though liberated from the doublings of doubt, he was, by the perverse paradoxes that marked his essence and his acts, more perfectly doubled than ever.

The submissive, asexual husband was now more submissive and asexual than ever. He did whatever his beloved Fenya told him to do. Not quite. She was a healthy woman, as outgoing as he was aloof, as talkative as he was taciturn, and she wanted the pleasures of the bed more often than the every three months that seemed enough for him. And that could lead to sharp exchanges.

"Living with you's like living with a blank wall," said Fenya.

"The trouble with you," replied Chikatilo, "is that you've gotten fat and lazy. Should I get you a stud horse?"

Her Andrei had never really forgiven her for the abortion.

He'd always said he wanted a large family, but she insisted the two they had was all they could afford. Fenya clinched the argument by asking him if he'd turned religious. But hadn't he told her how much he hated the idea of the doctors going inside her to kill their child? Things hadn't been the same between them since.

He could not be reproached for excessive lust, that she had noticed from the very first, on their wedding night when he "needed her help," as he called it. But this she had seen as proof of his delicacy, the shyness and bashfulness which had initially attracted her. He could not be reproached for drinking and smoking like many other Russian husbands. And he never wanted anything for himself, content to wear the same clothes all the time, his only indulgence newspapers, though he did sometimes economize even there, by visiting the public library. He was a man of simple tastes, with a fondness for raw eggs and herring, a serious person who allowed himself no distractions except the occasional game of chess.

No one could say of her Andrei that he hadn't given more than most to the building of communism. His newspaper articles so impressed the editor that he even offered Andrei a full-time position as a columnist. He had specialized in international affairs at the Institute of Marxism-Leninism. If you wanted to know what was going in the world, her husband was the man to ask.

And he could hardly be reproached as a father. He never raised a hand to the children. Never even raised his voice to them. And he enjoyed their unbounded respect, they'd always be quiet when their Papa was reading the papers in the evening. Of course sometimes their son would complain that his father had no eye for beauty and nice things. But children could not be expected to understand that their father was a man of the mind, with degrees in Russian literature, communications engineering, and Marxism-Leninism. Their Papa had made great strides in life—from the peasantry to the intelligentsia in one generation. From a terrible childhood to a peaceful family life. The children had been born in good times and had no idea what the words famine and war really meant. But for people who had spent their childhood in Ukraine during the Nazi occupation, no words had greater meaning than hunger and death.

He was a man who knew children and loved them. Loved them sometimes a little too much, as had happened in the seventies when they said he was bothering girls. It didn't make sense, he was too weak to satisfy even her, what would he have left over? Still, he had been touching some of them in ways he shouldn't have been, he'd admitted that. But that was years ago and, as the saying goes, even the sun's got spots on it.

Chikatilo turned the pages of his newspaper, which rustled in home's evening quiet. Sadat was assassinated in October. The socialist won the elections in Greece. The pro-Moscow communists had done badly in Greece but that was only to be expected, the contradictions of their society had not yet reached the critical stage.

In mid-November Brezhnev announced that, because of bad weather for a third year in a row, food remained the nation's greatest problem. Brezhnev was looking worse all the time, puffy with sickness and shots. There were rumors that the famous mystic healer Dzhuna was now paying regular visits to the Kremlin, only her powers keeping the leader alive. And the war in Afghanistan had not resulted in any quick and clear victory, almost two years now. At least on December 13 the Polish situation was put back in order, Solidarity crushed and martial law declared.

Chikatilo slept well. And though the screams of the schoolgirl or the lightness of a severed nipple on his tongue haunted his memory, they could not entice him to act, for month after month.

It takes time for the psyche's enzymes to break down transformational experience and structure a second self. Especially when that second self was so different from the first. One paled at the sight of blood, the other exulted in it. One cringed at a hypodermic needle, the other could jab a knife through a stomach wall. One was helpless before any offense, the other avenged a life of insult.

But the two selves also had a great deal in common. They shared the same memories, the same body, the same name. And perhaps there was even a third Chikatilo, the one who could see both of the others and knew he could be either. Chikatilo had divided like a cell, but was still held in the membrane of a single identity.

And all this took time. The days were measured for him as they were for everyone, by work, by home, by sleep. Things had taken a turn for the worse at work. He was starting to feel poisoned again. People had gotten to know him and come to dislike him. He wasn't personable, never looked anyone in the eye. The men, and the women too, didn't like the way he stood with the back of his hand on his hip. There was something feminine about the slope of his shoulders they didn't like— even in the army they had made fun of his body, saying he had the figure of a girl. And if that hadn't been mortifying enough, one day he'd gone off to take a leak in the woods and had masturbated when he was done. But his sergeant had seen him. And when Chikatilo came back all the soldiers roared with laughter and showered him with shameful names. He hadn't even seen the sergeant, that's how "blind" he was. Eyes and genitals had caused him suffering again. He still didn't wear glasses for fear of being called "four eyes." It was only when he married Fenya that he finally found the courage to get fitted for a pair of eyeglasses.

But if people were going to start poisoning his life again with their looks and snickers and intrigues, he didn't have to just stand there and take it, even if he could do nothing on the spot, insults always rendering him silent and inert. He had become a master of the genre of the letter of official complaint.

Like all art, it has, at the very least for the author, its there-peutic side.

He had written his first letter of complaint in his army days to protest being slapped in the face by an officer, even though Chikatilo himself would later agree that had been the best way to wipe the silly smile off his face.

It was during his military service that Chikatilo applied for membership in the party. Not "for a career" as Chikatilo scorn-fully put it, but out of "true Soviet patriotism" and an "iron faith" in the imminent global victory of communism. The boy who had drawn maps of the world emblazoned with the name of the communist party leader of every country and the youth who had marched and sung more stridently than anyone "and we shall die as a man in battle for that victory" was, in 1961, at the age of 25, accorded the solemn honor of full membership in the Communist Party of the Soviet Union.

He volunteered, an activist who gave of his time to edit wall newspapers, serve on the party's executive committee on physical culture and sport, inspect schools. That passion did not abate even after he married. Sometimes he would return home so exhausted Fenya would exclaim: "You look more dead than alive, what are you killing yourself for?" But he could not tell her what he had sensed early on, that it was better if his body and its desires were exhausted by useful work.

Nineteen eighty-one marked the twentieth anniversary of Chikatilo's membership in the party. He had proved his loyalty through action, service, sacrifice. It was the party that con-nected him to the world, to events at home and in the interna-tional arena, and that gave them meaning. The fact that in early 1982 the French had decided to socialize much of their econ-omy was not an isolated event but part of the larger dialectical weave of history. And when, after fifteen years as head of the KGB, Yuri Andropov resigned to assume a party post, that could only mean that he was being groomed to replace Brezh-nev, who could barely totter to the podium these days.

Andropov would put some iron back into life. And that would speed the inevitable triumph of communism. The imminence of a change of rulers allowed Chikatilo to indulge in one of his favorite fantasies, that—his talents and devotion at last recognized—it was he, Comrade Andrei Romanovich Chikatilo, who was asked to lead the Soviet Union into the future!

Chikatilo's first two murders had had a haphazard quality about them, as initial efforts often do. His intentions in both cases may have been only sexual. He had known that the cries of the terrified excited him, but had not known that it was murder itself with all its drama that was for him the supreme sexual act. Now he knew.

He knew that there was not one world, but two, as different as flesh and X ray.

He had the power that comes from the secret knowledge that only murderers can have.

He had not known about that power and secret knowledge.

And now that he knew, he wanted to know more.

The first two murders had been only rough sketches yet had contained all the elements that would mark Chikatilo's later crimes—the fear of eyes, the hatred of genitals. His first murder, of the nine-year-old schoolgirl Lena Zakotnova, had been performed by choking and stabbing, though the wounds had only been three in number and had not entirely succeeded in putting her to death. Still, he had found his weapons and his means. With the wild girl, Larisa Tkachenko, he had learned the ritual—a sincere attempt at normal sex, failure, insults, murder, sexual cannibalism, a little funeral of his own devising.

Yet an amazing transformation would take place between the second and the third murders. What was quick and crude became deliberate and complex. The murderer emerged full blown, and, as chance would have it, the time between the second and third murders was, almost to the day, nine months.

On June 6, 1982, he enticed a twelve-year-old girl into the

woods near a remote and dismal bus stop where the buses were forever breaking down, forever late. The Soviet system was still working for him. All it took was the most ordinary of questions—"Your bus late too?"—to start the most ordinary of conversations. He knew how to talk to children. He had been a teacher, he was the father of two.

Later, no one paid any special attention to the tall man with the glasses and briefcase who emerged from the woods and walked over to the station to rejoin the crowd. People would have been too tired or irritated to care—it was getting harder to find bread, milk, and potatoes, the buses were always breaking down.

Chikatilo did not pay them much attention either, except to observe if anyone gave him special notice. His colors merged with the grays and browns of the crowd, his newspaper with the other newspapers. Nearly all of them carried some sort of bag, from net bags known as "maybe bags"—maybe they'll have something in the store—to cheap, mass-produced plastic over-the-shoulder bags, some of which had foreign words on them in French or English. His bag was no different except that it contained clothes damp with fresh blood, for he had stabbed this girl, not three times as he had his first victim, but forty-one.

He may also have come to believe there was something to the age-old superstition that the image of the murderer is imprinted on the victim's eyes. It wasn't a chance he was going to take and anyway he had no liking for eyes. No one would find his image on what was left of that girl's eyes.

The party and the Soviet system rewarded the faithful. In late July 1982, Senior Procurement Engineer Andrei Chikatilo, who had been bothered recently by a touch of arthritis in his knee, was offered and accepted a combination of therapy and vacation at a workers' resort in the city of Krasnodar, meaning Red Gift.

But this was one benefit of the Soviet system Andrei

Chikatilo chose not to avail himself of. Instead, he went from train station to train station, sleeping on benches along with the other stranded passengers, using bathrooms that were no more than a slab of cement with three holes, no water, no paper, no separation into stalls. He would watch the vagrants, the winos, the sluts living their free and laughing life, waiting for the signal, the certainty, that one could be cut away from the herd. This was his vacation, his therapy.

Within three weeks he took three lives. A fourteen-year-old girl, a nine-year-old boy, and a girl aged sixteen followed him into the woods. If any image did indeed imprint on their eyes, it was of a murderer in ecstasy on top of them.

Oleg Podzhidaev was the first boy Chikatilo killed, setting a precedent and a pattern. Boys he attacked immediately as soon as they were alone in the woods; one stunning blow, tie their hands, a few shallow knife wounds to establish control.

When Chikatilo was himself a little boy, he had heroic dreams, idolizing the partisans who had fought the Nazis in the woods near his native village. The partisans had an expression—to take a tongue—which meant to find someone who had information and to make him speak. Now, in Chikatilo's fantasy, he was a partisan ordered by his stern commander to take the "tongue" into the woods, tie him up, and use his knife on him.

When, in the name of the partisans, Chikatilo ordered this first boy to stick out his tongue, the boy did what he was told, the instinct for survival and sheer terror even overcoming his natural repugnance when the man took his tongue into his mouth. He was a street kid, smart, he knew what these old homos wanted.

But not this one. The teeth that had taken a nipple now took a tongue.

And, as he would with nearly all of the boys, Chikatilo took the genitals with him from the murder site.

Chikatilo's wife was surprised that he did not look better

rested when he returned home, but the long nights in the train stations and the dramatic passion of the three murders had left him stunned and drained. What better place to rest than home, where, after a day's work, his wife prepared the evening meal while he studied the newspapers.

Despite the efforts of science and the occult, Leonid Brezhnev finally succumbed on November 10. The nation was embarrassed by the multitude of medals Brezhnev had instructed himself to be awarded, each of which, according to communist funeral custom, had been separately carried on a pillow of crimson silk. Two days later, as expected, former KGB chief Yuri Andropov took control of the party and country.

It was on December 11, 1982, early in the reign of Andropov, that Chikatilo committed his seventh and last murder of the year. Chikatilo was at a bus station on his way to visit his mother-in-law. Olya Stalmachenok, a ten-year-old music student, was on her way home.

Her death was the most horrible of the year's. There were more than fifty knife wounds, several to the eyes and, something he had never done before, savage eviscerations.

Seven children had gone with him into the woods because he could speak their language. Because their situation was the same—a bus or train delayed and any attempt to find out when it might be arriving met only with curses or indifference. Because it took so little to interest them—the promise of a shortcut, a video, something to eat.

But the real reason was that young people can see so clearly. They just look and see and know. And they had gone with him because they had seen who he was, a defenseless man.

C H A P T E R   7

I'm going to kill that Kostoev!" screamed the murderer, Volodya Storozhenko. "I'll tear his throat out!"

The investigator left the room. He had been assigned to deal with the details of Storozhenko's confession after Kostoev himself had caught and cracked the serial killer in the summer of 1981. The investigator telephoned Kostoev, who said he'd be there as fast as he could.

Storozhenko was furious because he had just discovered that Kostoev had arrested his brother. The fact that his brother had been involved in several serious crimes did not cross his mind at that moment; there was no room for logic in the rage of betrayal.

During the interrogation Kostoev had come to rather like Storozhenko, a good-looking young man of twenty-eight, with strong Slavic features, simpatico. Still, Kostoev knew that at heart Storozhenko was a very dangerous person who had robbed, raped, and murdered a dozen women.

Kostoev left in such a rush that he even forgot his hat. This was not only a matter of cutting a good figure at all times, it was very cold in the city of Smolensk in the winter of 1981. In the spring the Russian Attorney General's Office had instructed Kostoev to assume control of a murder case that had the city of Smolensk in terror. Women were afraid to go to the factories, production was falling. And the more than two years of killings were an insult to the party's authority and ability to maintain order.

Carefully orchestrating the manhunt, Kostoev caught the killer in four months' time. Of the twenty women Storozhenko thought he had killed, eight had survived, and one had, in the fury of sexual and homicidal assault, somehow been able to perceive and remember her assailant. Still, the only charge Kostoev could bring against him was one case of rape and attempted murder. Kostoev would need a confession.

Storozhenko was a tough guy who'd already done time, and who wore the tattoo of the snow leopard on his shoulder, insignia of the Russian outlaw. The tattoo on his chest, a pale-green angel with its wings extended in flight, looked like a needle-and-thread job done in prison.

Kostoev could read the signs, he knew about the snow leopard, he knew about guys like Storozhenko with their muscular necks and reckless bravado. His strategy would be an attitude of such absolute confidence that it could even offer hope if a confession were made, the sort of false hope known in Kostoev's profession as a "rubber nipple."

"This isn't my specialty," said Kostoev, "but I do have the feeling that there are certain agencies of our government that could use a man like you. The international situation's very tense right now, Khomeini, Reagan, the Pope."

Storozhenko was listening intently.

"I've heard all sorts of stories," continued Kostoev. "Sometimes they sentence a man to death then issue a false execution certificate. He gets a new name, sometimes even a new face through plastic surgery, and then he's sent abroad."

Though attracted, Storozhenko was resisting now because it had become clear to him that the price of this new life was a full confession. But, judging by the way Inspector Kostoev acted, it seemed he had more than enough evidence to convict him to no less than life in prison for the rape and attempted murder of the eight women who had survived.

"Do you know any foreign languages?" asked Kostoev.

"I could learn," answered Storozhenko.

Having staked his bet, Storozhenko confessed to twenty rapes, twelve murders, and eight attempted, and then, in his spare time in the cell, had set about mastering English.

As soon as Kostoev arrived, hatless and fresh from the cold, he ordered Storozhenko brought to him and then, over the guard's objections, ordered that they be left alone in the room.

Storozhenko was still enraged, dangerous. Kostoev showed no fear because he felt none.

Challenging Storozhenko to maintain eye contact, Kostoev chided at the verge of anger: "So, you want to kill me because you found out I arrested your brother, you'd have been happier if I told you before? I had you transferred out of a cell where the other prisoners were planning to do to you what you did to those innocent women." Storozhenko could no longer meet Kostoev's gaze and his head began to incline.

"And I made sure you were given good conditions here. Is that why you want to kill me, or is it because I'm seeing to it that your wife and child are taken care of?"

His head down, Storozhenko wept as he said: "I'm sorry."

Then Kostoev ordered the same investigator to resume the interrogation.

Seeing the man that same evening, Kostoev asked: "Well, how did it go?"

"Like silk."

"What did he say?"

"He said, I was ready to kill that Kostoev, tear out his throat, but he just played me like a fiddle. He's not human, he's a devil!"

After writing Storozhenko's indictment, which would surely lead to his execution, Kostoev took a vacation with his family.

Two weeks later, calling in to the Russian Attorney General's Office in Moscow, Crimes of Special Importance, Kostoev learned that he was being sent to the city of Rostov on the Don on a "small matter of corruption."

"It's nothing, nothing, you'll be done in two months," said Dimitrov, who had been Kostoev's Attorney General and protector in the Vladikavkaz days and who was now the Attorney General of Rostov.

"Your interests aren't involved?" asked Kostoev.

"No, no, it's nothing, a low-level bribe."

That hardly seemed a fitting assignment after trapping and breaking a serial killer like Storozhenko, but orders were orders. He took a room at the Hotel Rostov. Looking straight from his balcony, he could see the antenna on the KGB building and, looking down, the top of a young weeping willow.

After he had acquainted himself with the case in his usual deliberate fashion, Kostoev began questioning the man who had extorted the bribe, Andrei Natolok, an investigator with the Rostov Attorney General's Office who had dropped a case in exchange for some repairs on his car, swapping justice for fenders. It may have been the wish to mitigate his own fate by helping the investigation or the refusal to go down alone, but Natolok incriminated a few others. That set off a chain reaction, each person betraying two or three more who in turn yielded others. The entire judicial system from the cop on the beat to the judge on the bench was riddled with corruption. A case could always be dropped or a sentence reduced if the price was right.

Several things became apparent quickly. Corruption in Rostov reached higher up in rank and farther back in time than anyone, himself included, could have imagined. He found he needed two assistants, then five, until that number finally reached fifteen. This case wasn't going to take weeks but months and maybe years. Room 339 at the Hotel Rostov was going to be home for quite some time, if a narrow room with a short and narrow bed could be called home.

Sooner or later all clues in the Rostov corruption case led to Anatoly Kamsky, the city's deputy attorney general. A brilliant detective, connoisseur of the law, and masterful interrogator, Kamsky was so perfectly corrupt that he often did not even perform the service for which he had been paid. He was feared by everyone for he had power and no scruples.

It took all the rest of the year to build a case against Kamsky that could withstand any attack. In the meantime Kostoev received word that Kamsky was offering big money for anyone who killed him. He began sleeping with a pistol and going out with two or more of his men.

Since he was investigating corruption within the judicial system, Kostoev could not allow suspects or prisoners to be held in the jails or prisons of that same system, where they could easily be gotten at. Only the KGB offered the neutrality and hermetically sealed isolation that the situation required. The KGB proved willing to assist Kostoev. Yuri Andropov, the former head of the KGB, was now running the country and had made the cauterizing of corruption a high priority. The KGB allowed Kostoev to have his prisoners held in their isolation prison and to use one of their interrogation rooms, Number 211, to question them.

Room 211 proved lucky for Kostoev. Of the nearly seventy people involved in the corruption case, all had confessed. But now it was time to take on Kamsky himself, an adept at the game. And, at fifty-four, Kamsky was the more experienced man, Kostoev only thirty-nine at the time.

Kostoev had been impeded just long enough in arresting Kamsky for the gold and diamonds to disappear from the hiding place behind the toolshed in Kamsky's garage. With his thinning light hair, coolly contemptuous eyes, and cigarette holder, Kamsky reminded Kostoev of a Gestapo officer. In fact, a deep background check on Kamsky had revealed that, as a youth, Kamsky had supposedly collaborated with the Nazis, even receiving a motorcycle for his services. In the famine years right after the war, he had stolen a woman's bread ration card, which meant that she starved to death and he didn't.

No sooner had they sat down in Room 211 than Kamsky, fearing electronic bugs, began attempting to bribe Kostoev by using his fingers to indicate the offer. He started with one hundred thousand, then quickly jumped to two.

Kostoev laughed. "Not enough, you're worth more than that."

Finding his fingers insufficient for the task at hand and, still fearing their conversation was being monitored, Kamsky grabbed paper and pen and wrote: Half a million.

"That won't work with me. There's only one possibility," said Kostoev.

"What's that?" wrote Kamsky.

"The only thing that can mitigate your sentence is a full confession."

"I've got nothing to confess," wrote Kamsky.

"Then why are you offering me bribes?" said Kostoev in a suddenly loud voice.

"I haven't been offering you any bribes!" said Kamsky, bursting into speech and ending Day One of what would prove an arduous interrogation, one of the three in which Kostoev failed to obtain a confession.

In a sense, it did not matter to Kostoev that Kamsky would never confess. He had more than enough against Kamsky—he would receive no less than twenty years, and might even be executed. It was more a matter of professional pride. Still, what mattered most was that Kamsky and some seventy others, one having even become a Soviet Minister in the meantime, were on their way to being punished. Those people were simply bandits who had found the juiciest pickings, and the safest hideouts were in the judicial system.

In Rostov Kostoev was famous and hated. Only the few

honest people in the judicial system regarded him without fear and loathing. The common people credited Kostoev with improving their supply of provisions. Whenever large quantities of food suddenly appeared in the stores, it was Rostov's firm opinion that Kostoev was planning another wave of arrests and the big shots were dumping their private supplies of coffee and sausage on the market so as not to be caught with a big inventory that might prove difficult to explain.

One December afternoon Kostoev noticed an athletically built man in his thirties crossing the low, dim lobby of the Hotel Rostov. As soon as the man turned and Kostoev saw his dark hair and snub nose, he recognized a colleague from his own department in Moscow, Volodya Kazakov.

"Volodya, what are you doing here?" asked Kostoev.

"You haven't heard about the maniac?"

"No. Come to my room, we'll have a drink, and you can tell me."

While Kostoev got out the glasses and the bottle and some food to chase the vodka with, Kazakov told him what he'd learned so far. "There's a maniac killing women and children all over the province, Shakhty, Rostov, something like twenty different cases. I've been assigned to merge them into a single operation."

"And how's it going?" asked Kostoev, pouring the vodka, his guest's first.

"The problem is that the Rostov police have arrested a retarded nineteen-year-old who's already confessed to ten of the murders. And so, what the Rostov police are saying is who needs a single operation if they've already got the killer?"

"Good luck," said Kostoev, raising his glass. "You'll need it down here."

C H A P T E R   8

Nineteen eighty-two had been a year of experiment and discovery for Andrei Chikatilo, his nature revealed to him through enactments.

Patterns had been established that would vary little over the next eight years. His victims would be boys, girls, and young women. There would be many runaways and retarded among the children and teenagers, they were easier to convince, grateful for help in the maze of a local transportation system with which they were not familiar. Attuned to the signs of disorientation, Chikatilo would cull them from the crowds at train stations or bus stops and, on one pretext or another, convince them to follow him into wooded areas, "forest strips." There he would inflict multiple stab wounds, usually thirty to fifty. Nearly all victims would suffer mutilation of the eyes. In the case of teenage girls and young women, breasts and nipples were removed either with his well-sharpened knives or his teeth. The uterus would be taken with such precision that every surgeon in Rostov province would become a potential suspect. With the boys he would either sever their genitals entirely or only remove their testicles, leaving the empty pod of the scrotum. In some cases these amputations were performed while the victim was, though not conscious, still alive. In no case were any of the severed body parts found at or near the scene of the crime.

Chikatilo had committed his first murder in Shakhty when he killed the nine-year-old schoolgirl in his secret house on Border Lane. His second took place in Rostov when he crossed to the left bank of the Don with the wild girl in the claret-red jacket. Then he had gone on to commit the seven murders of 1982 which spelled out his deepest desires to him. Chikatilo had followed the oldest adage of philosophy, and had come to know himself.

There was nothing new for him to discover in 1983, now there would only be variations on a theme, the satisfaction of specific lusts. Perhaps the crazy two-step he performed that year was itself an acknowledgment that the first great series was over—in 1983 Chikatilo killed first in Shakhty, where he had taken a life for the first time and then he struck in Rostov, where he had slain his second victim. He repeated the process: his third victim in 1983 was killed in Shakhty, his fourth in Rostov.

By late December of 1983, Chikatilo had killed as many as he had the previous year, seven, the two years in perfect balance like the scales of Libra, his birth sign. But then, on December 27, Chikatilo was returning from Moscow with a truckload of linoleum. When they were only a short distance from the warehouse, Senior Procurement Engineer Chikatilo suddenly ordered the driver to let him off at an out-of-the-way train station. Chikatilo instructed him to proceed to the warehouse and make the delivery of the linoleum himself. It didn't make sense to the driver. They were almost to the warehouse outside of Shakhty. After they made the delivery, he could give Engineer Chikatilo a lift right to his door. And, besides, the Senior Procurement Engineer was supposed to sign off for the delivery, not the driver.

But Chikatilo would hear none of it, apparently having some other sudden and urgent business. Indeed it was. The fifteen-year-old boy who followed Chikatilo into the woods suffered more than seventy knife wounds before the root of all evil and suffering was severed from him.

Perhaps in all things just measure can be exceeded. The linoleum shipment had come up one roll short.

The woman clerk who checked the delivery against the invoice made an official complaint against Chikatilo to the management, and a criminal complaint as well was not out of the question.

The driver had probably taken one roll for himself before he made the delivery. Or maybe the woman who checked it needed some new flooring at home. The main point was that he had no friends at the factory who'd be glad to wink at something like this. On the contrary, he had nothing but enemies at work. People who disliked him, people glad to do him a bad turn. Now they had found a way of both humiliating and dismissing him—petty theft.

If a criminal complaint were brought against him, Chikatilo would automatically be expelled from the Communist Party of the Soviet Union. It didn't look good if party members went on trial.

He had never been more furious in his life. Chikatilo began killing as he had never killed before. On January 9 it was a teenage girl, on February 21, his oldest victim, a forty-five-year-old woman, a drifter, half drunk when their paths crossed.

The very next day, February 22, 1984, Chikatilo was informed that a criminal complaint was being brought against him in connection with the missing roll of linoleum. Not only that, a check of past records had also indicated some irregularities with a shipment of car batteries.

The worst of it was that he *had* taken one of the car batteries, fully intending to pay for it, even though there was no good reason he should, because many times he had used his own private car to pick up a small shipment, and so in fact he was at least owed a battery for his trouble. Nevertheless, he was going to pay for the battery but just hadn't gotten around to it. He was becoming more forgetful all the time.

Summonses started arriving from the police. He didn't answer them, he was too busy murdering. He killed in March, he killed in May, though the May killings were more a matter of chance than intent. Chikatilo had made a date with a woman whom he saw from time to time. She would allow him to perform oral sex on her while masturbating himself to orgasm. But on that day, the woman brought her eleven-year-old daughter with her. And even that would have been alright, because the daughter knew her mother's ways and ran off up ahead. But this time the woman was not patient with him and made wounding remarks, which meant that he had to run after the daughter with a hammer after he had silenced her mother.

Later that spring, Chikatilo was openly told at work that he should begin seeking other employment.

He took a leave and began looking for work. This required frequent trips back and forth from Shakhty to Rostov on commuter trains. The khaki-colored cars with their high steps are so plain inside that the faces of the passengers are always strangely distinct, even if they are sleeping. Many suffering faces. Faces of almost comical simplicity. Foxy peasants. The innocent faces of the young. And of the young who are not innocent.

And the ones that look loose, or lost.

The trusting, eager eyes of the demented.

Answering two imperatives, in the late spring and early summer Chikatilo murdered and sought work. By the end of July, he had killed nine people, in some cases adding insult to injury to avenge the insult now being done to him. The insult he now added was to remove, in one piece, the upper lip and nose which had begun to strike him as genital-like, then to place them in the victim's mouth or stomach.

Still, most evenings he would return home, eat dinner, read the paper. Andropov had succumbed to kidney failure on February 10, 1984. His replacement, Chernenko, was a compromise choice who would be permitted the honor of being the last member of the Brezhnev team to die in office. Andropov had supposedly been grooming a young Politburo member, Mikhail Gorbachev, who, years earlier as a regional party boss, had welcomed Andropov when he arrived at a local hot springs for a kidney treatment.

Sometime in that year 1984 Andrei Chikatilo ceased entirely having sexual relations with his wife. Though infrequently, he had, until then, been able to be intimate with her in bed, to touch her and be touched. Now that was no longer possible for him.

No one had ever lived a more perfectly double life than he, but in a double life the secret side always takes its toll on the side shown to the world. And the secret side had its own laws. And by those laws he was no longer able to have any physical connection with Fenya, though that may only have increased his adoration of her.

By August 1, he had found a new position as Procurement Engineer for a factory in Rostov and by August 2 had killed a sixteen-year-old girl in the city of his new employment. The summonses were still hanging over his head, infuriating him. Five days later, he killed a seventeen-year-old girl on the left bank of the Don, a murder whose location and scenario—failed sex, insult, homicide—matched that of his second victim, the wild girl in the claret-red jacket, except that the number of wounds and savage excisions exceeded anything he had done to her. When in the middle of the month he was sent on his first business trip to Tashkent, the capital of Uzbekistan, closer to China than to Rostov, he killed two women within the space of five days. By the end of August the total was fourteen.

It had been a poisoned summer. Dismissal, a criminal complaint, the danger of being expelled from the party just as it was on the verge of rejuvenation. It was also the summer of the second poisoned Olympics, for Soviet athletes boycotted the games in Los Angeles. To do otherwise would have been to admit that the incursion of Soviet troops into Afghanistan had been mistaken.

And all that poison had to be vented so that he could know some peace. And when he had found that peace, he would kiss the neck of the young woman beside him on the grass, sometimes tenderly, sometimes with a last passion that left a mark.

Then he would rise with a creak in his knee, which had been acting up again lately. Rubbing his knee to remove the grass stains and ease the pain, he would look down at the body. Sometimes, despite all the wounds, the young woman would still be breathing.

By then he was adept at avoiding blood when he opened the lower abdomen, fatty in many women. But there was no avoiding blood when he went inside to sever the ligaments which held the pear-shaped, pear-sized uterus in place.

Having put the sperm where it belonged and having cleaned up after himself, he would walk away into the blue summer darkness, spent and at peace, smiling as his teeth took their initial grip on the uterus, the truffle of sexual murder.

On September 13, 1984, one week after his fifteenth murder of the year, Andrei Chikatilo caught the attention of two Rostov police detectives, Akhmatkhanov and Zanosovsky. They were on night patrol near the central bus station in Rostov in connection with the case now known as "Operation Forest Strip"; even though the police and Attorney General had obtained confessions from the retarded youth, the murders had continued.

In his report, Akhmatkhanov stated:

I was on patrol at the bus station with Captain Zanosovsky from the First of May precinct of the Rostov police. . . . We were in plainclothes. . . . While outside the station, Zanosovsky pointed out to me a tall man, approximately 180 cm in height,

lean, about 45 years of age, whose features were very reminis-
cent of those in the composite sketch. He was wearing glasses,
no hat . . . carrying a brown briefcase. Zanosovsky told me that
he had seen this man before when he had been on patrol without
me at the Suburban Bus Station and considered him suspicious.
We agreed to keep the man under surveillance. . . . Bus No. 7
which goes from the train station to the airport arrived. Working
his way through the crowd of passengers, the suspect boarded
the bus. Zanosovsky and I boarded the bus after him. While
observing him, I was struck by his strange behavior, he seemed
very ill at ease and was always twisting his head from one side
to the other . . . I had the impression that he was trying to make
sure that he was not being followed. Having noticed nothing
suspicious, the suspect attempted to make contact with a girl
who was standing beside him. She was wearing a low-cut dress
and he couldn't take his eyes off her breasts. While we were
following him, this citizen touched a woman's legs causing a
conflict with her. After three stops he got off the bus. He crossed
to the other side of the street and stood with the passengers
waiting for a bus going in the opposite direction. . . . When the
bus arrived, we all boarded. . . .

On the bus he would stop by women and stare at them, try
to make contact with them, and press up against them. . . . He
took a seat by a woman who was sitting by the window and
attempted to strike up a conversation with her. . . . When the
woman got off the bus, he followed her. Evidently, he was not
able to come to an agreement with her and she walked
away. . . . The suspect walked over to a store where there were
groups of women standing. He kept walking up to one group then
another for about 15–20 minutes. Then he went on foot to the
next bus stop from where he took a bus to a train station. There
he spent about 20 minutes sitting next to a sleeping woman then
went on foot to the Main Train Station. . . . He kept walking over
to groups of women and listening in on their conversations.
Then he went up to the waiting room on the second floor. . . . He

spent about an hour walking around the waiting room, stopping by women and looking intently at them. . . . He stopped by a bench on which a family was sleeping. One of them, a girl of about eighteen, was sleeping in such a position that her legs and underwear were visible. Stopping five feet from the sleeping girl, the suspect stared at her. When the girl's father straightened out her clothing, the suspect walked away. . . .

Then a young woman sat down next to Chikatilo and, after a short conversation, she placed her head on his knees. He covered her with his jacket while she performed oral sex and he fondled her breasts. A short while after she left, Chikatilo rose and went to the Central Market where, after a long and sleepless night, he treated himself to his favorite food, herring, though of the inferior sort from the waters of Japan. It was then and there that he was arrested for licentious behavior in public and as well on suspicion of the Forest Strip murders.

The two plainclothesmen were convinced they had found the killer whose looks and actions not only matched the profile, but whose briefcase proved to contain a well-sharpened knife, two lengths of rope, and a jar of Vaseline. He also had an ID folder which resembled that of a "non-staff police assistant."

Chikatilo's blood, type A, did not match the semen found on the victims, which was AB. Blood and semen were known to be always of the same group. The arresting officers were dismayed when this information reached them, everything else had seemed so perfect, but there was no disputing hard scientific evidence. The Rostov police did, however, alert Kostoev's colleague from Moscow, Vladimir Kazakov, about Chikatilo. Kazakov was still in Rostov on assignment from the Russian Attorney General's Office. His task, to unite all the related murders in Rostov Province, had still not been accomplished, the main obstacle being the insistence by both the police and the Rostov Attorney General's Office that they had already caught the killer, or, rather, the killers. Having obtained a confession from the first mentally ill youth they arrested, they were briefly stymied when the murders continued. But quickly enough they solved this problem as well, deciding that the subsequent murders had been committed by friends of the original suspect to cover the trail. More mentally ill youths were arrested, more confessions obtained.

Kazakov dispatched Inspector Moiseev to question the new suspect, Andrei Chikatilo. Moiseev questioned him for two days, the sixteenth and seventeenth of September, while Chikatilo was serving fifteen days' administrative arrest for licentious public conduct. In the course of their conversations Moiseev learned that Chikatilo suffered from "sexual weakness," no longer slept with his wife, and had committed child molestations in the past. But as Chikatilo himself said, "The fact that I suffer from sexual inadequacy is not so important for a man my age, almost fifty." Moiseev also noted that Chikatilo was in the habit of sleeping at train stations, had often been in Rostov in the past on business, especially on Tuesdays and Thursdays (days favored by the killer), and had once owned a house at 26 Border Lane in Shakhty. Moiseev gave instructions that a closer check be run on Chikatilo, then had to return to more pressing matters, the nearly year-long fight to free the mentally ill youths, the "half wits" as they'd come to be called, and to unite all the related cases, the latter finally being achieved on October 8, 1984. That, however, was largely a meaningless victory as long as the "half wits" were still in custody and considered the prime suspects.

By then Chikatilo had served his fifteen days of administrative arrest but, instead of being released, was sent to Novoshakhtinsk to be checked out in connection with the murder of an eleven-year-old boy, Dima Ptashnikov, a case that was not yet part of Operation Forest Strip. Dima had last been seen with a tall man wearing glasses and carrying a briefcase.

The police of Novoshakhtinsk questioned Chikatilo's wife and daughter, searched his car, and took a sample of his blood, which did not match in type the semen found in the body of the eleven-year-old victim. Apparently, they did not call in any of the people who had seen the boy on the day of his disappearance with a tall man in glasses to identify Chikatilo. They may not have done so because they had already used more than the ten days legally allowed them to question the suspect and his family, take his blood, and search his car. The police found themselves in something of an awkward position, for it would seem that they were holding a law-abiding citizen and communist. But then fortune smiled on the police of Novoshakhtinsk. They had made inquiries of the police in neighboring towns— did they have anything on a certain Chikatilo, Andrei Romanovich? And it turned out that Chikatilo was a wanted man, in connection with the theft of socialist property, one roll of linoleum and a car battery. Chikatilo was promptly remanded to the custody of the Shakhty police.

After a brief stay with the Shakhty police, Chikatilo was sent to Novocherkassk Prison to await trial. While incarcerated there, he learned that what he had so long dreaded had finally taken place—on November 23, 1984, he was officially expelled from the Communist Party of the Soviet Union.

On December 12 of that same year his case came up for trial. The charge of stealing the linoleum was dropped but he was given a year of corrective labor for the theft of the battery. In practice, that meant that twenty-five percent of his salary would be deducted each month for one year. But considering that he had been in jail since September 13, three months, the court ruled that every day Chikatilo had served would count for four. His sentence was thus considered already to have been served and Chikatilo was released.

At least there had been some justice—he hadn't done time for the linoleum.

CHAPTER 9

Though none on earth could sense how great, change was in the air as soon as Mikhail Gorbachev became the leader of the Union of Soviet Socialist Republics in March of 1985, as the Russian winter began yielding to the riotous Russian spring. His head anointed with a charismatic birthmark, his suits well cut, Gorbachev radiated dynamism and modernity. A contemporary communist, not another old man with one foot in the past and the other in the grave.

Gorbachev was going to rebuild the house of communism, the house whose foundation Lenin had laid but whose structure had been designed and built by Joseph Stalin. But how many of those I-beams could be safely removed?

A Soviet citizen did not have to be as diligent a reader of newspapers as Andrei Chikatilo to know that there had been no announcement of victory in the war in Afghanistan, which had been dragging on for more than four years now. Boys were still coming home in coffins and the ones who returned alive were addicted to narcotics and violence, or had just quietly lost all hope. Perhaps it was enough to support Cuba with millions a day and to fund insurrections the world over, maybe they didn't need Afghanistan. And at home all the systems seemed to be breaking down, from transportation to justice.

By the time Inspector Kostoev was packing his things in

Room 339 of the Hotel Rostov, the weeping willow had reached even with the stubby concrete balcony. He was leaving, but Kazakov was staying. Kazakov had gotten into the habit of dropping by to see Kostoev in Room 339, for vodka, canned sardines, a boiled egg, bread, whatever had been scraped together for the evening meal. He had consulted often with Kostoev on his problems, which were maddening. The Rostov police and the Rostov Attorney General's Office were sticking to their position, that the "half wits" they kept arresting were the ones responsible for the more than twenty sex murders that had taken place in the province since 1982. Every time there was another murder, they would arrest another "half wit"! And, most maddening of all, that position was bolstered by the fact that murders seemed to have ceased.

Kazakov continued his war with the Rostov police and Attorney General's Office to free the retarded youths, but as of May 1985 no essential progress had been made. Kazakov bombarded Moscow with reports of grievous sloppiness on the part of both the local police and inspectors who trampled crime scenes, lost evidence, and were satisfied with confessions that would almost surely prove to have been wrested by force and coercion.

The simplest links were not functioning. The police were supposed to turn over all missing persons reports at once to the Attorney General's office inspectors. Not only were they not passing them on, they weren't even investigating them themselves. There was no need now to trace down the fate of every runaway and drifter, they had Yuri Kalenik, a twenty-one-year-old retarded carpenter, who had confessed to ten of the killings, the others having been done by his friends. Kazakov knew that the real killer had to be laughing up his sleeve.

On May 31, 1985, Kazakov wrote to his superior, Deputy Attorney General of the Russian Federation Namestnikov, stating that he thought it necessary that a "competent investigator be sent to Rostov Province to evaluate objectively all the 'pros' and 'cons' of Kalenik's guilt." The response did not come until October, possibly because in Russia things nearly always move very slowly except when they go lightning fast, or because it was decided to give the situation a little more time to develop.

In any case, on October 25, 1985, there was a high-level meeting in Moscow, the primary players being the Attorney General of the Soviet Union, the Attorney General of Russia, the Attorney General of Rostov Province, the head of the Soviet Police Ministry, and the head of Rostov's police. The declared subject of the meeting was: "The implementation of measures to improve the investigation by the Attorney General's office and the police of the killing of women and children in Rostov Province."

After much mutual recrimination as well as serious discussion, a decision was reached—that the case be transferred for "further investigation to the investigative branch of the Russian Attorney General's Office and be headed up by a highly qualified investigator, one who has specialized in investigating complex cases of premeditated murder, Comrade Issa Magamedovich Kostoev."

Kostoev was present at the meeting but did not speak. Knowing that it would be a great case to solve, Kostoev also knew that it was going to be just the way Kazakov had put it in one of his dispatches—either long, slow, and painstaking, or quick through sheer luck.

On November 10, 1985, Inspector Kostoev submitted his formal written acceptance of the case, assigning it No. 18/ 59639-85, and then left at once for Rostov.

PART III

CHAPTER 10

The rain and mud of Russian autumn were just giving way to the snows of Russian winter as Inspector Kostoev arrived in Rostov on the Don. There in the fertile "black earth" zone even the mud had a dark, rich viscosity. The snow was not heavy yet, the progress of winter measurable by the hats Russians wear. Knitted wool caps will be worn for as long as possible until the stinging air requires a shift to fur, but even then Russians will delay lowering the fur earlaps, that sign of last surrender. Regardless of the weather, Kostoev himself preferred snap-brim felt fedoras or even, upon occasion, a derby.

He checked into the Hotel Rostov where he requested and received 339, the same room he'd had during the corruption case. At least it was familiar. And this time he had no illusions of a short stay.

His first order of business was to divide his team of fifteen investigators into two groups, one to be stationed in Rostov, the other in Shakhty, the two areas where the most murders had occurred. He obtained the basics for them—office space, cars, desks, typewriters, safes. Then they all could get down to the laborious reading of the files. By November 1985 there were twenty-three known murders dating back to 1982 and there were several thick volumes on each. There was no way to know a case without reading the files and there was no way to read the files quickly. Especially since they had been banged out on manual typewriters with thinning ribbons on tired carbons.

It would be slow at the beginning, and it should be slow. You only get one shot at organizing the work properly, then things go into motion and take their course. Some inspectors and detectives just came in, flipped through the files, issued orders, and that was that. But that was not the way Kostoev did his business. He took his time.

Unlike the others on his team, Kostoev not only had to study the material on the murders but that on the "half wits" as well. The first one was arrested in late 1983; after that he and the other retarded youths who lived together in a special school kept being rearrested and rearrested. In the meantime more than two years had passed. The actual killer could only be emboldened by such laxity.

The Rostov Police and Attorney General's Office were united against him, both still insisting, But we've got the killers!

Kostoev let them both know exactly where he stood: "I took over the case on orders from the Russian Attorney General's Office. Now's not the time, but someday the people responsible for imprisoning those kids for two years are going to have to answer for it. In the meantime, I'm securing their release."

But that was easier said than done. He would have to fight the criminal justice system before he could even think of going after the criminal. And, unlike his opponents, he was going to have to prove his case.

Kostoev went back to the files. But he had other sources to draw on as well. There were the tales of Nasrudin, the wise fool of Islam, which he had heard from his father as a child, his favorite of course the one in which Nasrudin plays detective.

Nasrudin's wife says to him, Go to the market and buy two pounds of rice and I'll make you pilaf for dinner.

Pilaf was his favorite, so he went right to the market and brought the rice home and only then left for work.

When Nasrudin returned that evening, he found his wife fast asleep on the couch. The pilaf pot on the stove was empty.

Nasrudin woke up his wife and said: What happened to my dinner?

The cat must have eaten it, said his wife.

Nasrudin grabbed the cat and put it on the scale. It weighed two pounds. So, said Nasrudin, if that's the cat, then where's the pilaf? And if that's the pilaf, where's the cat?

Reading the files about the "maniac" and the "half wits," Kostoev smiled as he found the perfect equivalent to the cat-and-pilaf tale. Now, armed with the proper papers, Inspector Kostoev went at once to see Alexander Yanishkin, Attorney General for the Province of Rostov, the sole person able to order the release of the "half wits."

"Did you ever hear of a man with three balls?" asked Kostoev.

"Never," replied the Attorney General.

"Well, a man was killed in the Tselina district and his balls were cut off. They were found at the scene and sent to the morgue. Then the police arrest another half wit. Did you kill him, they ask. I killed him, he says. How? With a knife. Did you cut off his balls? Yes, I cut off one of his balls with a knife.

"Then they take him to the scene of the crime so he can show them where and how did it.

"And where did you throw the ball you cut off?

"Over there, he says.

"They go over, and what do they find—the ball. But two balls have already been sent to the morgue, there's a receipt for them. So, either one ball was brought back to the scene to falsify a case or the man had three balls to start with, you tell me."

When the half wits were at last released, Kostoev was able to return to the files with but a single purpose now, to come to know the killer. The Storozhenko case kept coming to mind, the most recent, the most similar. Even the form of the situation was similar, a serial killer, a case going nowhere, Kostoev called in.

Was this another Storozhenko, another underworld type with a snow leopard tattooed on his shoulder and a flying angel on his chest?

One thing was certain—this one was better at killing than Storozhenko who had left twenty women for dead, though only twelve in fact were. This one had assaulted twenty-three and not one had escaped alive.

There were twenty-three known victims, some only skeletal remains. Other such remains might well have been classified as accident victims, so that the local police involved would not have to launch an extensive investigation that would require genuine effort and might not even succeed.

In the Storozhenko case, he had had a live witness who could describe her assailant, here he had no one and nothing. Someone had once seen one of the victims with a man wearing dark glasses and there was a footprint of a large shoe, 10, 11, found at one of the sites. The angle and force of some wounds indicated that the man was tall and strong. The killer was a tall strong man who wore glasses. Or at least had on the day he was seen. That is, if that man was indeed the killer. And even the shoeprint wasn't a hundred percent clue, it could just as easily belong to some clumsy flatfoot.

Since arriving in Rostov, Kostoev had already heard several hilarious accounts of police ineptitude. In one, a police squad had arrived at a murder scene where they discovered a tire print. The chief ordered a plaster cast to be made of it. But it turned out that they had forgotten the plaster. Alright then, ordered the chief, just saw out the whole piece of ground and bring it back to the lab. For a moment no one had said anything, then someone politely pointed out that the tire print was in sand, which could prove difficult to saw.

Kostoev enjoyed that tale in particular. The local police and inspectors from the Russian Attorney General's Office were natural enemies and enjoyed nothing more than a laugh at each other's expense.

Kostoev was running the Rostov office himself, having placed Shakhty under Kazakov, who had spent two years battling for the half wits' freedom and was therefore quite familiar with the case. Kostoev would also rely heavily on Inspector Yandiev, who had proved his worth during the Rostov corruption case.

On the short side, always neatly dressed and cleanly shaven, Yandiev did not have Kostoev's panache and drive, but he was every bit as dogged in pursuit. His black hair thinning on top, Yandiev was ordinary in appearance, which served him well for he liked to get out, walk around, talk with people. He did have one unusual feature, his large green eyes which had an emerald luminosity. Perhaps it was because Yandiev spent so much time in morgues—in time even becoming able to eat in the morgue cafeteria—that his dream was to retire to the high mountains and raise bees.

The main clue in this case was the absence of any clues. No physical evidence to speak of, no witnesses, no victims who'd miraculously survived. The crime sites were clean. That could mean that the killer had some working knowledge of police methods. Either from having read about them, or, more likely, from having worked in some capacity with the police. Every precinct had a good number of paid agents who provided information and other services. Some of them were criminals, like Storozhenko, who had taken an active part in the hunt for himself, even making a few rubles in the bargain.

Storozhenko had robbed his victims, this one stripped them of all their belongings and clothes. Maybe he kept souvenirs. But more likely he was just taking intelligent precautions. There were always at least 3,000 missing persons in Rostov Province at any one given time and a naked body takes longer to identify. That time works for the killer, the first day or two being nearly everything in a murder investigation. Then the weather eats clues and memories fade.

Not only did this killer seem familiar with police procedure, he appeared to have some knowledge of human anatomy as well, able to remove one victim's uterus on a moonless night. Sometimes he bit off breasts and the tips of boys' tongues. But none of the body parts the killer sliced off with his well-sharpened knife were ever found at the scene. In some instances, the remains of a campfire were found in the general vicinity of a mutilated corpse. There was no reason to think a killer like this would stop short of cannibalism.

Compared to this one, Storozhenko was normal. He only raped, robbed, and murdered grown women.

The women this one murdered were mostly drifters, sluts, whores who'd do whatever you wanted for a bite to eat, a couple of drinks, a few rubles. And that only proved that anything those women would do was not what the killer wanted.

The photographs of the murdered children were the most shocking and enraging. The shock wore off, the rage remained, becoming a sediment of determination.

Kostoev had never seen such hateful wounds. To rape a child and then to kill that child is understandable. It has a logic. A man has a sexual weakness for children. For a time he fights it but then he succumbs. He kills the child to avoid punishment, the same reason Storozhenko had killed the women he raped.

But the wounds this one had inflicted had not only been to kill. Some of the wounds were very light, especially on and around the throat and chest of some of the boys. They had been inflicted early, to subdue the victim, and to bring the killer a taste of power, narcotic of the impotent. And some of the other wounds—the mutilation of the eyes and excision of genitals—were inflicted after death or when the victim was hovering near death.

Semen was found in the vaginas of the little girls he killed and in the anuses of the boys. In some cases the killer had clearly had more than one ejaculation, semen also being found on the clothing. This was a man who jerked off on dying children.

To help him understand the killer's mind and motive, Kostoev ordered a translation be made of Krafft-Ebing's classic work *Psychopathia Sexualis,* which had been known to the whole world since the late nineteenth century, but which had never been published in puritanical Soviet Russia. In the Lenin Library in Moscow, Kostoev unearthed a special limited edition of a volume published in 1929 by the NKVD, as the KGB was known under Stalin. Entitled "Crimes and Criminals of Western Europe" by its author, B. Utevsky, who may have wished in so naming his book to cast no aspersions on his own society, it did nevertheless contain instances both in the Soviet Union and abroad of behavior that far exceeded normal murder.

One chapter was called: "24 Murders On Sexual Grounds With Dismembering And Disfiguring Of The Corpses." That was close to what he was working on. Another case concerned a practical cannibal who made belts of his victims' skin and offered them for sale. There were no limits to what people could do. The criminal was always breaking new ground, always ahead of the inspector, until the very end, the capture.

None of the books answered Kostoev's real question, why a person goes so far. But the reading was useful because it expanded Kostoev's knowledge of crimes committed out of some fathomless dream, not rage, fear, or greed. To maim and kill for sexual pleasure implied stupendous arrogance—the murderer believed anything was allowed him. And that arrogance must also have assured that he was too cunning and careful ever to be caught.

Nothing was ever found at the scenes of his crimes. In some instances the victim's hands had been tied but not even a fiber of rope or cord was ever discovered on or near the victim. The killer needed something in which to carry the rope and the knife to the scene, maybe he carried spare clothes, too. He'd probably carry one of those slightly sporty, plastic over-the-shoulder bags or the kind of hard-sided briefcases known as a "Diplomat." But nearly every man in the country carried one or the other.

And nearly everybody carried a knife. There were always times when a person on the road couldn't find anything to eat; a smart traveler would have some bread and meat with him, and a knife to cut them with. The killer needn't be nicely dressed for the sluts to go off with him, but some of the children he had murdered were of good family, and would not have gone off with a stranger unless he seemed neat and respectable. How did he tempt them? What exactly did he say?

And the specialists were helpful. Soviet science had some knowledge of these people, the psychology of sexual murderers. Actions could be classified. Onanism. Vampirism. Necrophilia. But they were as abstract as the killer, only a tall moving shape with glasses and briefcase.

A shape that hunted in train stations and bus terminals. In the end, their first profile Kostoev's team drew up of the killer said all that they realistically knew of him:

"A man between 25 and 55, tall, muscular, with Blood Type AB. Shoe size 10 or larger, wears dark glasses, neat in appearance. Carries a "Diplomat" or other bag which contains sharpened knives. Suffers from a mental disorder originating in perversions of a sexual nature (onanism, pedophilia, necrophilia, homosexuality and sadism). He may also suffer from impotence, has knowledge of human anatomy.

"Most probably initial point of contact with victim: commuter train stops, railroad stations, and bus terminals. Exhibits intelligence in performing his crimes. His employment may allow him to travel freely."

Kostoev divided the hunt into seven basic lines of pursuit:

—Persons previously convicted for a murder of a sexual nature, sex crimes and homosexuality, including those currently incarcerated.

—Persons registered as patients in psychiatric institutions, narcotic treatment centers, or receiving care from specialists in sexual pathology and venereal diseases.

—Workers in the railroad system, soldiers in military units stationed in the area of the murders.

—Employees of cultural, educational, athletic, and preschool institutions.

—Owners and operators of motor vehicles.

—Owners of video technology and horror film videos, and also frequenters of video arcades.

—Former law enforcement personnel, dishonorably discharged.

In addition, Kostoev instructed his team to scour the files for all similar cases of murder throughout the entire Soviet Union for the last twenty years. All missing persons in Rostov and adjoining provinces would have to be checked out as well.

An immense number of people. Which meant that it could be almost anybody. And that dictated the method. At the first operational meeting of the entire team, Kostoev said: "There are no clues, no witnesses. And so we have to use the process of elimination. That means slow, hard work. Every suspect has to be checked so carefully and thoroughly that there is not a single shred of doubt left about him.

"The worst mistake we can make is to let the killer slip through our filter, because once he's through, he's gone."

Now on the streets of Rostov people were wearing knitted caps and some few even went bareheaded.

It was April, time for action.

"I'll put everyone on alert, the whole force will be working for you," said the Deputy Chief of the Rostov Police with a generosity that did not fool Kostoev for a second.

"No," said Kostoev. "Give me twenty or thirty men who'll do this full-time, nothing but this."

Kostoev won the point if only because, according to law, in investigations of this sort the police were subordinate to the Attorney General's Office. The responsibility of the police was to gather information for Kostoev and to perform the tasks he indicated.

The police might be subordinate to him but that didn't mean in the least that Kostoev could do without them. They would be the ones in the field, hanging around train stations, working their agents. And he was already off on the wrong foot with them. But whose fault was that? What was he supposed to do—congratulate the local authorities who had been busy wringing confessions from the mentally retarded, while the corpses piled up throughout the Province of Rostov? Was he supposed to find that exemplary professional behavior?

And besides it wasn't as simple as that either, there were some good men on the Rostov police and some of his inspectors were incompetents.

The Rostov Police might have been subordinate to the Attorney General's Office but that did not mean that the police were powerless. They would have the considerable power of controlling the flow of information that reached Kostoev, deciding what he saw and what was kept for police use only. Kostoev knew that the police's ability to withhold information as they saw fit went back to Stalin's time, when the police and the secret police had been merged. Major Burakov of the Rostov Police was to be in charge of the file index at staff headquarters, keeping track of the color-coded cards, for neither the police nor the attorney general's office had a computer, another consequence of Stalin, who distrusted computers.

The net was cast, as fine as it was broad. While waiting for the first catch to come in, Inspector Kostoev made a tour of the murder sites in the company of a young policeman who drove him from one to the other. In a double-breasted topcoat, scarf, and snap-brim hat, he tramped through fields that had the faintly ammoniac smell of earth coming back to life. How had the killer shepherded them on? Did they talk on the way? Or walk in a comfortable silence?

Kostoev stood in the tall silence of the trees where the killer had stopped, having found a place that he liked, that suited him, where he felt safe and secure. Kostoev tried to imagine exactly what the man did, with what expression, making what sounds, at what speed. But it was all still a blur.

From nearly every grove and forest strip Kostoev could hear the sounds of a railroad, hoots, clacking—commuter trains, freight trains, an express.

Nearly all the victims had been found in the vicinity of rail or bus transportation. But some were found as much as three miles from the nearest form of transportation. Had the victim and killer walked all that way? Did the killer have a car of his own, or was he someone who worked with a car, like a taxi driver, not always the best citizens?

If it was more than three miles, you'd have to figure there was a vehicle involved, anything less and you could safely rule it out. But that distance was like the killer, indeterminate, neither quite one thing nor the other.

As Kostoev walked out of a high stand of acacias he said to the young policeman something he would repeat again and again to everyone working on the case: "It's the trains, the trains, if the police ride the trains in plainclothes, just sit there and read a book or a newspaper and keep their eyes open, he'll fall into our hands. And sooner rather than later. But only if they keep a sharp eye out."

That was the maddening thing. He could instruct the police to have outlying train stations watched. But the police would decide which men to dispatch there. And then it was up to those men to decide what was more important, standing around a train station or having a beer, buying a chicken.

Then Kostoev got into the police car and headed back to

Rostov. He was quiet now. He never liked talking while in any form of conveyance, car, subway, or plane. He knew he would be coming back to some of those places. Some of those groves and forest strips spoke to him more than others. It is not only killers who return to the scene of the crime.

There were some intriguing flickers of possibility right from the very start. On April 14, 1986, a young boy was approached on a commuter train by a man who showed him a red police ID, then took him into the woods near the tracks where he had sexual relations with him. The man was 40–45, athletically built, with a swarthy oval face, gold front teeth, and the tattoo of an anchor on his left wrist.

The age was right. There was a police connection, just as there had been in the Storozhenko case. The situation was right, trains, woods. Now the face was not a perfect blank but had a shape and a skin tone. Three or four of the man's front upper teeth were entirely encased in gold, fitting for a man who bit off the tongues of boys and the breasts of women.

There was one key difference—a victim had now returned alive. But that had to happen sooner or later, no killer could be that perfect.

The man with the gold teeth and the green anchor on his wrist struck again eleven days later and this time his intended victim was a young girl. She too survived and her description of her assailant matched the boy's. She was also able to supply one additional detail—this time the man had been carrying a "Diplomat" briefcase.

A composite sketch was drawn up and distributed. But the suspect just faded away. He had struck twice, then vanished. Maybe he was only passing through. Or maybe he left Rostov at once after committing his crimes. It hardly mattered. What mattered was that the police who had been assigned to cover the trains had not been on their toes.

Kostoev had his two basic groups broken down into seven

subgroups, each responsible for one line of pursuit. Those groups interfaced with the police, which supplied them with information, the most interesting of which was supposed to flow directly to Kostoev. Some lines of pursuit were harder than others. Large numbers of troops were stationed in Rostov and the outlying areas. But any investigation of military personnel had to be done through the offices of the Military Investigators. Reading the files on patients in mental hospitals was unlikely to produce quick results since many patients had been in and out of a variety of institutions, making it difficult to determine whether a given individual met the most important criterion—could he have been in such and such a place on such and such a day?

The homosexuals were the easiest group to go after. Since any form of homosexuality, even with mutual consent, was a crime punishable by up to five years of incarceration, many of the local homosexuals had been convicted and as a result were on file. In fact, as Kostoev discovered, there was even a separate file on known homosexuals within the party, government, and judicial system. Their favorite meeting spots were also well known, a men's room by a restaurant on the left bank of the Don, the area near the Academy of Music and Art.

The killer was clearly a homosexual, a sadistic pedophile. The boys he killed nearly always had his semen in their anuses.

The heat was put on the world of the "light blues," as Russian homosexuals call themselves. Kostoev's position was clear and direct: "There'll be no peace for you until the killer is caught. We're going to turn this town upside down. It would be better for you if you helped us. Let us know who's aggressive, who's got problems like that."

The pressure produced quick results, and an education for Kostoev. One "light blue" would pay young naval cadets to form a circle around him, beat him with their belts as he stood naked, screaming his way to orgasm. Another called himself "Silvia" and only used the feminine grammatical forms, even the past tense of a verb revealing the speaker's sex in the Russian language. Some of course wore women's clothes, most preferring to look chic though there were those who liked to look like old Russian grandmothers with kerchiefs and big flowered dresses. One of that type had even found himself a job as a men's room attendant, a job often given to old women who mop the floors and hand out toilet paper for small tips.

But the most unforgettable of all was Irene. The only son of an important railroad official, he dressed as a woman and worked as a nurse in the local hospital. There he helped bring one handsome young man back to health in a great drama of rescue, gratitude, and passion. The young man could hardly be blamed for falling in love with his nurse, Irene, she was so beautiful, her hair done so well, her nails so elegant. And the clothes she wore when she was out of her nurse's uniform were as stunning as the light of love in her eyes.

The young man was finally released. Still believing Irene was a woman, he began seeing "her" outside the hospital. When the force of feeling became irresistibly great, the young man made a discovery that momentarily horrified him, but only momentarily, for Irene was not going to allow anything to thwart the great love of her life. Before the young man knew quite what was happening, Irene had spun around and deftly placed him where she could compete with any woman.

And apparently Irene had given her young man the ride of his life, for he quickly came to share her views on the unimportance of minor obstacles to great passion. After a time their idyll was shattered by harsh Soviet reality—the young man was called up for military service. But that only raised the romance to a higher pitch. Irene wrote him often, every letter a drama, the kind that resonate in the heart for days. Finally, the great moment came. "I don't know how you'll feel about this," wrote Irene, "but I'm pregnant with your child."

Irene was the best of them all! She took it all the way.

In the first great sweep, over four hundred homosexuals

were brought in and forty-eight were indicted. For rape. Sex with a minor. Homosexuality itself. Some could not bear the terror of exposure in a society where their sexuality was not only a crime but a disgrace. A young man named Victor Cher-nyai, a waiter at the Don/Volga restaurant, hung himself almost the very day the hunt started.

When not interrogating the most interesting suspects and overseeing the work of the Rostov and Shakhty groups, Inspec-tor Kostoev would go back to the files, especially those con-cerning murders which had initially been viewed as possibly related to "Operation Forest Strip" but which, for one reason or another, had been rejected as the work of another killer.

One case caught Kostoev's interest. The year before, on August 27, 1985, an eighteen-year-old vagrant by the name of Inessa Gulyaeva had been murdered in the woods near the bus station in the town of Shakhty. The picture on file of Gulyaeva showed a buxom young woman with a broad face and contrast-ingly thin brows that were highly arched. She had been sexu-ally active since the age of twelve and had quit school after the eighth grade, refusing to work, preferring a life of sex and drinking. Inessa Gulyaeva had left home in April 1985 and had not been heard of until her naked body was found under a covering of pine needles and rags in late August.

The autopsy revealed that Gulyaeva had been rendered unconscious by a tremendous blow to her solar plexus that had almost killed her. Death, however, was caused by strangu-lation. The victim's mouth was filled with dirt, there were strange patterns of scratches inflicted after death on the right side of her back and her left buttock and hip. Approximately ten wounds to her vagina had been made by a sharp instru-ment no less than nine centimeters in length.

One graying hair had been found between the middle and ring finger of her right hand.

The case had not been merged with "Operation Forest Strip" because the killer's "handwriting," as the wound pattern and general behavior of the criminal was called, did not seem to match. Knife wounds to the vagina were nothing uncommon. And none of the usual signs of disfigurement were present.

But, thought Kostoev, maybe the killer had been interrupted, maybe he hadn't had time to do everything he wanted. The woods where he had taken her were close to the bus station where he had no doubt picked her up. And somehow the places—Shakhty, a bus station, a forest strip—seemed like "his."

Kostoev decided to turn this stone over and see what came scurrying out.

The first thing he learned was that on the very day of her murder Inessa Gulyaeva had been released from three days of administrative arrest for "vagrancy and living a parasitical way of life." Released at five o'clock, she was dead a few hours later. The Shakhty police records indicated that when she was released, Inessa Gulyaeva had no money at all, just her ID. She was wearing a white dress.

It also turned out that one of the policemen who worked in the holding cells had suddenly remembered an important errand just after Inessa Gulyaeva was released. That policeman had also been seen going off into the woods with Inessa a short time later. Inspector Kostoev had indicated that people dishonorably discharged from the police were to be among the prime suspects but, by extension, that would also have to include those who should have been discharged or would soon be. Kostoev called the policeman, Sergei Kolchin, in for questioning.

"When you left the police station at around five o'clock on August 27, 1985, did you meet with Inessa Gulyaeva?"

"No."

"What did you do?"

"I went for cigarettes."

"Did you have sexual relations with Gulyaeva while she was incarcerated?"

"No, I didn't."

"We have information to the contrary."

"What do you want," asked Kolchin, "a lie or the truth? If you want me to say I killed her, alright, I killed her."

"But you didn't go running after her?"

"Is that what you want me to say?"

"You were seen going off into the woods with her near the bus stop station."

"Alright, alright, I banged her in the jail and I banged her in the woods but I didn't kill her."

Kostoev believed him. Police records indicated that Kolchin could not have been in the places where the other murders had been committed. Kostoev released Kolchin, who was later dismissed from the force in connection with another matter, the theft of some grain.

The materials of the case also contained a report from Rostov's Deputy Chief of Police, V.I. Kolesnikov, who stated:

". . . on August 28, 1985 I was informed that the corpse of an unidentified woman showing signs of a violent death had been found in the vicinity of the bus station in Shakhty. I went at once to the scene of the crime. I noticed piles of garbage at the edge of the forest strip, near the asphalt walkway. My eye was caught by what seemed a rolled-up bundle. Pulling it from the garbage, I saw that it was a woman's dress. Thinking this might be the victim's clothing, I instructed a policeman to bring the clothing in as evidence. When the victim's identity was established and I inquired about the clothing I had discovered, it turned out that it had been lost due to the sloppiness on the part of our men . . ."

But Inspector Yandiev, his green eyes glowing whenever he uncovered new leads, had also been active during this time. He had found a "parachute"—a legitimate reason to hold a suspect while you get what you want from him—for one of the main crime figures in Rostov province, who had yielded a valuable piece of information. On the day that Gulyaeva was

brought for autopsy to the morgue in Shakhty, one of the forensic experts, left alone with her had, under the influence of
alcohol, found her charms unblighted by death.

Yandiev called him in for informal questioning. The expert
had an alibi for the time of the murder and hotly denied any
improprieties with Gulyaeva's corpse, but Inspector Yandiev
put more credence in the terror in the man's eyes than in his
words. Inspector Yandiev decided not to bring a case against
him, satisfying himself during his not infrequent visits to the
morgue that the fear of God had lodged securely in the man,
who would go running at the very sight of Yandiev.

They had filled in the last hours of Inessa Gulyaeva's life.
She had been "banged" in the jail and "banged" in the woods
before she ran into a killer who knocked her out cold with one
tremendous blow to the solar plexus. But she must have regained consciousness at some point, long enough to struggle
and tear a single gray hair from her assailant's head. Then he
had strangled her and had been stabbing her vagina with a
knife when something had probably put him on the alert, a
sound, a voice too close. He had then dragged the corpse
further away where he covered it with rags and pine needles.
Found the next day, Inessa Gulyaeva's body was taken to the
morgue, where despite its wounds it still proved attractive to
the forensic specialist for whom the boundary between life and
death had long since blurred. They knew everything about the
victim's last hours except who had made them the last.

CHAPTER 11

Kostoev and his men were solving all the wrong murders. They were solving them speedily, sometimes brilliantly. But none of the murderers was the one they were being paid to find.

They gave particular attention to any murders that might be *his*. The woman found dead, naked, and bereft of one breast in the neighboring town of Bataisk was, therefore, of some interest. That interest mounted to great excitement when similar murders kept occurring in the same general vicinity. The fact that the murderer in Bataisk proved just as elusive as the one in Rostov only seemed further to indicate they could be one and the same.

By early 1987, Kostoev and Yandiev were working closely together. Yandiev was sent to Bataisk to head an on-the-spot team with a Rostov police detective, Syzenko, a good but very competitive man, with whom Yandiev enjoyed working.

Always taking pleasure in clear and neatly rendered diagrams, Yandiev marked the four points where the murders had occurred on a map of Bataisk, connected the points, and determined that a certain area of intersection could be established and should be searched.

The area in question contained factories and dwellings. One factory reported that a young engineer had recently disappeared. Yandiev and Detective Syzenko went to his home where he lived with his young wife and his mother.

When they arrived, Syzenko said, "I'll take the wife, you take the mother," and had said it so unexpectedly and abruptly that Yandiev did not have time to react.

Syzenko's game was obvious—a wife might have grievances, but what mother was going to turn in a son?

But Yandiev had mastered the rare and difficult art of talking with people. He knew what worked and what didn't. There was no need to come right to the point. And even when you finally got on the subject, it was better to come at it from the side.

"I'm from Rostov," said Yandiev, "and so I'm not up on the situation."

"They say my boy raped and killed women, I don't know, they suspect he did anyway."

"Do you believe your son could have done it?"

"No."

"I've never seen your son," said Yandiev, "but I have seen his wife. She's very nice. I can't believe that a young man with a nice young wife like that would do things like that. But they're searching for your son now. And if he tries to run away again, they could shoot him. They could kill an innocent person. I can prevent that if you tell me where he is."

When Detective Syzenko returned from questioning the wife, he was beaming with triumph and pride. "I've solved it. It was him."

"And where is he now?" asked Yandiev.

"That's the one thing I don't know."

"But it's one thing I do know," said Yandiev, with only the hint of a smile.

The young man was apprehended and confessed, his spirit broken by the knowledge that his own mother had turned him in. Four murders had been solved but not the right ones.

Spirits were not flagging yet, but no one was more aware

than Kostoev himself that it had been more than a year since he had arrived in the mud and snow of a Rostov November. He had been there so long now that he had even begun fixing up Room 339 a little more to his liking, the large TV now directly across from his bed, the night table out of the way to make more space in what was a narrow room to begin with.

Unless something of special urgency was happening, Kostoev's workday and that of the other inspectors ended somewhere between eight and ten in the evening. They took turns gathering in each other's hotel rooms to have a bite and a few drinks. Yandiev was married and at the end of the day could go home to a wife, children, food cooked in a kitchen, not on a hot plate. But when the stories had been told and the bottle finished, Kostoev would be alone in 339 where the very top of the weeping willow was now just above the balcony.

In the dark he would try to imagine exactly what the killer did to his victims, in what order, what was done in delight, and what in fury. On some victims' necks signs of hard kisses seemed to have been found.

But was the killer still killing? Every murder that seemed to bear his signature had turned out to be someone else's. Had the killer stopped killing, aware that there was an all-out manhunt for him now? It was no secret in the city of Rostov that the same Inspector Kostoev who had shaken all the graft out of the judicial system and who was even credited for markets suddenly bulging with sausage was back in town. If the killer was like Storozhenko and had connections with the police, he would have been one of the first to know that the case had been turned over to the Russian Attorney General's Office and was being headed up on the spot by Kostoev. Some killers can refrain when they feel in danger.

Or maybe he was killing elsewhere, it was a big country. Bulletins had gone out to all the other fourteen Soviet republics to report any similar cases within the last twenty years, with special emphasis on the last five. But Kostoev could hardly count on reliable information flowing to him in a timely fashion from the hinterland. It's always easier to classify a body, especially a skeleton, as an accident victim and not have an unsolved murder hanging over the department's head, "hangers" as such cases were known.

He could rely on some of his inspectors and a few of the police. During the bribery case, Kostoev had learned that inspectors from the Attorney General's Office could be as corrupt as the police and now he was learning they could be as inept. Once he had sent two men out in one direction and then later that day had himself headed off in quite the opposite direction. Driving along, he noticed two familiar-looking men sitting at a table beside a small truck that dispensed beer from a squat khaki tank attached to the cab. Kostoev ordered his driver to pull over.

"So this is how we search for the killer!" roared Kostoev. "Not only in the wrong place but drinking beer!"

Then he could not help himself and burst out laughing, this was, after all, Russia, not Austria.

Kostoev sometimes worried that the killer had been arrested for another crime in the meantime and was now safely in jail. Everyone arrested in the entire Soviet Union in the time since August 1985, when Inessa Gulyaeva, the last known victim, was murdered, would have to be checked. Another colossal task. Over time Kostoev had grown convinced that the case of Gulyaeva was the work of "their" killer and had the case officially connected with the others in Operation Forest Strip.

If the killer was still in the province of Rostov, had he changed his method of disposing of the bodies? Could he be concealing them more carefully than before, possibly even burying them?

That meant that the Missing Persons were even more important than ever, both in Rostov province and in those adjoining. All that work had to be done, it was absolutely necessary, but still Kostoev somehow knew that in the end that wasn't how they were going to catch him. They would catch him on the trains. Or, if a great miracle happened, one of his victims would escape alive and be able to put a face on that shape, that tall silhouette carrying a briefcase.

Though Kostoev would sometimes be temporarily torn from Rostov to assist on an urgent case elsewhere in the country, when he was in Rostov, and that was most of the time, he had worked out a definite routine. On the way to his office, he would check to make sure that the police were in fact watching the stations and riding the trains. Some of the police he knew by sight, some he could tell by type. The first thing he would do when arriving at his office was to check what crimes had occurred during the night. If there had been anything of special interest, he would of course have been awakened, but you couldn't depend on anyone but yourself to decide what was important and what was not.

Kostoev would then summon the group heads for a report on their progress. He would take the most promising materials, study them, and the following day issue any modifications of their lines of pursuit that had struck him as necessary. If any especially interesting suspects were in custody, he would interrogate them himself. There were the usual number of false confessions in which Kostoev found himself doing the opposite of what he usually did—instead of trying to elicit a confession, he'd be trying to punch holes in one.

That was what happened when Kostoev interrogated a young man who had attempted to rape a boy. When people had been drawn by the victim's cries, the rapist had dashed away and jumped a fence but had been apprehended soon after. Kostoev "worked" with him for five days.

Anyone caught committing a sex crime was a very likely suspect and Kostoev bore down very hard, his voice booming, his confidence relentless and overwhelming.

Finally, on the fifth day, the young man burst into tears.

"Yes, I killed a boy, and a girl, on the left bank of the Don."

And the murders he named were two with which Kostoev was familiar. Kostoev pressed him for details and the young man provided them. But there was something about his story that bothered Kostoev. Usually, the murderer can add some fresh detail, but this one was only telling him what he already knew.

"Did anyone question you before me?" asked Kostoev.

"Yes, a cop with red hair up on the third floor."

"Uh-huh," said Kostoev, with a knowing grunt that also meant the interrogation was over for the day.

He went up to the third floor and found the red-headed policeman in question.

"Did you interrogate the suspect?" asked Kostoev.

"Just a little."

"Who gave you the right? Did I instruct you to do it?"

"No," said the red-headed policeman.

"Let's go to his cell and see who he's in with."

And, to no great surprise of Kostoev's, the young man was in a cell with two men of the very sort who, for a few rubles, are glad to apply physical pressure on a suspect to confess.

"That's all you people know," thundered Kostoev. "Feed a suspect details, pressure him to confess. Those tricks don't work with me."

The young man was dropped as a murder suspect but indicted for the attempted rape of a minor. But new suspects appeared in view, succeeding each other quickly, each raising a hope only to dash it. The blood on the sack found in the home of a fireman known to be hostile to women when drunk proved only to be the blood of a pig he had stolen and killed. And some of the dentists who were questioned in connection with recent dental work on a few victims turned out to be stealing state gold, issued for the filling and encasing of teeth. Firemen were arrested for pigs and dentists for gold, but the killer was still invisible.

Kostoev was smoking too much. Rostov, famous as a tobacco town since the last century, manufactured its own
brands and cigarettes were never in short supply. Harsh
coughs racked his chest and he was bringing up too much
mucus. One of these days he was going to have to quit.

But not quite yet. Cigarettes were one of the few pleasures
of a life alone on the road. They made waiting more pleasant,
thinking easier. And there wasn't much other satisfaction to be
had.

"You want the killer, I'll give you the killer! It's my husband,
he's the cruelest man in the world!" screamed the woman with
the fury of those who have been wronged and are ready for
revenge.

When she finally quieted down, the woman had an interesting story to tell. Her husband had formerly been with the
police. "I don't know if he's killed anyone," she said, "but I do
know he's capable of it, he's capable of anything!"

"Why do you say that?"

"The other day we were having sex and all of a sudden he
pulls out this huge dildo made of wax and rams it into me so
deep I was all torn up inside and had to go to the hospital."

The husband was called in for questioning. Studying for an
advanced law degree, he was not only not intimidated but
indignant about this violation of his private life. He was especially reluctant to provide samples of his blood and semen, but
soon enough came to the realization that it would be better to
be eliminated as a suspect in Operation Forest Strip than to
remain one. His blood and semen were of a different type than
the killer's, and he could not have been in the places where
various killings had taken place.

The cavalcade of sexual oddities continued to pass before
Kostoev's eyes, sparkling with the pleasure of new discovery
and the hope of a lead. Men were caught propositioning youths
in the traditional Russian baths where men steamed them-

selves while beating themselves with bundles of birch twigs to quicken their circulation. Some were indicted, some were released, none was the one.

Rumors of a man performing strange experiments behind locked doors reached Kostoev's ear, but he proved only an inventor covetous of his patents. More interesting was a psychiatrist and professor at Rostov University's Medical School. Alexander Olympievich Bukhanovsky by name, he was one of the very few people in the Soviet Union who had specialized in transsexualism and was said to have played a significant role in several cases of sex change. Bukhanovsky was checked out "operatively," meaning that he was never called in for questioning but rather his whereabouts at certain key times were verified. Bukhanovsky passed through the filter with no problem, and would have dropped from view if not for a later connection with the Rostov police whom he served as a psychiatric consultant on the "Forest Strip" killer.

As spring approached, Kostoev realized it would soon be time for him to make his midyear report to headquarters in Moscow. He could report colossal efforts—4,000 mental patients had been checked, 680 sex offenders, 480 previously convicted of sex crimes. The KGB had supplied information on all those people in Rostov province who owned video players and every last one of them had been questioned. And working with the State Motor-Vehicle Inspectorate, the GAI, 147,807 vehicles had been stopped, their plate numbers noted, the drivers' name and license recorded.

He could also report gross negligence on the part of the local attorney general office's inspectors who lost physical evidence—belts, train tickets, purses, sweaters, cigarette butts—as if that were their principal task. But no matter what successes and shortcomings he reported, he could not report that the killer had been apprehended, and so by regulations was required formally to request that the investigation be extended for another six months, the period between July 1 and December 31, 1987.

The Rostov police were also busy with paperwork. They had sifted through the data they had gathered, organized it, and published it as an "Information Bulletin on 'Operation Forest Strip.'" The bulletin contained breakdowns of victims according to sex, age, occupation and according to the wounds, damage to the right eye, damage to the left, damage to both, genitals taken, not taken. There was a special category for "Signs of Sadism" which included the cutting off of the nose and part or all of the upper lip, the biting or cutting off of the tips of boys' tongues, bites on buttocks, cigarette burns.

There were categories for the type of knife used, signs of self-defense, the presence of semen in the body or on the victim's clothing, a list of items missing from the victims. The murders themselves had been broken down by year, season, month, and day of the week, the killer seeming to favor Tuesdays and Thursdays, with Saturdays in third place. The time elapsed between the actual murder and the finding of the body was noted. In many cases only skeletal remains had been found, and ultimately were sent off to forensic experts who specialized in the reconstruction of faces from bones and shreds of evidence. The Bulletin also contained a list of those who had come under suspicion, the twenty-two main figures being given in larger letters, whereas forty-four lesser figures were listed in smaller print. Ninth among those listed in large print was Chikatilo, Andrei Romanovich, who had been "detained in 1984 at the Rostov Train Station for licentious behavior for which he was convicted and sentenced. No connection proved with Operation Forest Strip. Blood Group A."

Summer brought panic back to Rostov. Parents were afraid to let their children go to the small sandy beaches on the left bank of the Don. Rumors ran wild—children had been snatched from school and, now that school was out, they were being snatched directly from the street, the playgrounds, the beaches.

The Jews of Rostov prayed that the killer be caught and not prove a Jew—there'd be pogroms in a minute. The old blood libel, that Jews sacrificed Christian children for their rituals, was alive and well in the south of Russia. The Armenians of Rostov prayed that the killer not prove Armenian. There was no particular myth about Armenians, nor would one be needed to launch a drunken, spontaneous slaughter. And those who were of mixed Armenian and Jewish blood, of which there were a good number in Rostov, prayed with especial fervor.

Kostoev had prayers of his own, a detective's twisted prayers. That the killer be alive, not dead. Well, not sick. And that he would soon, cruel as it was to think, kill again so that they could catch him at last.

Kostoev had won the goodwill of the people of Rostov during the corruption case—when the markets were suddenly flooded with coffee and sausage as big shots, fearing arrest, divested their holdings. But Kostoev lost every ounce of that goodwill in the summer of 1987. As usual, the beaches along the Don filled with swimmers, the cafes along the Don with revelers, and the forest strips with couples. But summer's pleasures were not to be had in peace that year—Inspector Kostoev was buzzing those woods in a helicopter, and every couple spotted in the act were immediately reported to a ground crew with a four-wheel vehicle who interrupted the lovers no matter at what stage to demand IDs.

Now Kostoev's name was cursed as earnestly as it had been praised in the old days of the corruption case. The people of Rostov were angry, not only because he was ruining their pleasures, but because the killer had yet to be caught. The killer kept every parent's heart edged with fear, causing them to whisper the terrible prayer of parents, let it be any child but mine. The people of Rostov were angry because the new era of glasnost had only revealed how much they had been kept in the dark all those years about crime, which wasn't even supposed to exist in their near-perfect society. There had been some public announcements about a killer loose in Rostov but they had always been dry and official, which only made the rumors all the wilder. Now, with the new freedom of the press, it was becoming plain that the killer was far worse than they could possibly have imagined.

Kostoev had talked to the parents of the slain children. He knew what it meant—all the rest of their lives would be spent in a pain and grief much worse than that of parents whose children had died from accidents or disease.

The bitter sediment of disappointment had started to twist the lips of some members of the team. Kostoev could see it at the daily meetings and the nightly drinking bouts. Some of the investigators were starting to lose heart, lose interest. Not Yandiev. They both ran on confidence.

Now there were tensions in the group, jealousies, hurt feelings, grievances never aired. Some of them resented Kostoev's style, in which they saw more than a touch of the generalissimo. Yet Kostoev himself noticed that it was never the good workers who were resentful. And any of them with eyes to see would long since have noticed that he was harder on himself than he was on any of them. He demanded more from himself because he expected so much of himself. If they didn't have the courage and high spirit to live life like that, so much the worse for them.

Still, nerves were getting raw, too many hopes had gone sour, the tautness of intent was being lost. He wasn't in such great shape himself. He was smoking more and coughing more, some of the coughs so deep he was even surprised that his lungs went down that far. And though he had fixed up Room 339 in the Hotel Rostov to suit himself, the difference between a can of sardines opened in a hotel room and dinner in your own home, the sound of your children's voices coming from the other rooms, was infinite.

* * *

The Soviet Air Force also made its contribution that summer to Operation Forest Strip. Aerial surveillance maps of all related areas were provided and studied for hours in Kostoev's headquarters both by him and the other inspectors. They knew the killer rode the trains and the buses; but where was his most likely point of origin? Maybe the maps could help with that.

Everything helped but nothing helped enough. No clear pattern emerged when the various points of the murder sites were connected.

And why wasn't the killer killing, the weather was good?

Perhaps he'd had a human moment, realized what he'd become, and hung himself. God forbid.

Kostoev slammed his fist on the table and shouted at the daily group heads meeting: "In the original profile it says that the man is an onanist. We've been on this case almost two years and I haven't interrogated a single onanist yet. You better bring me in one live onanist and bring him in fast!"

Crestfallen, irritated, even a bit sympathetic with Kostoev's impatience, the group heads left the meeting and immediately put out the word that the top priority was, for the time being at least, onanists.

Finally, one very indignant onanist was brought kicking and protesting into Kostoev's office. "If the policemen who beat me aren't punished, I'm going to make a formal complaint," said the man, who was in his late twenties.

"But why did you resist arrest?" asked Kostoev.

"What right did they have to arrest me? There was nobody around but them, who was I bothering?"

"But why not do it at home?" asked Kostoev.

"I like it in the woods. And it's my dick, goddamnit!"

By now Kostoev was laughing so hard that he could only wave the suspect out of the room.

Kostoev's wrath began to prove more effective than even he himself might have hoped. The next morning there were two unhappy-looking young men waiting in the corridor to be questioned by him, four the next morning, three the next, a confession being wrung from one by Yandiev, who used the aerial photography supplied by the Air Force to pinpoint the man enjoying his vice behind the wheel of his car, flashing the door open when a woman walked past. Every day there were more and more until Kostoev could no longer bear the sight of that loneliest tribe.

"Get them the hell out of here, I never want to see another one again!"

Kostoev thought he could detect a note of mockery in the killer's silence. Though all the many prisons and labor camps throughout the Soviet Union were being checked for anyone arrested in the period since the killer's last known killing, part of him believed that the killer was at large. His arrogance must be boundless now that he had killed so many without being caught. But he was clearly intelligent, too, that characteristic had gone right into the very first profile. He could change his tactics to ensure his own safety. He was a meticulous man, never a witness, never a clue. He might even be able to desist for years, though that was unlikely. By now he probably thought he had a right to his pleasures.

Sometimes when Kostoev walked the streets of Rostov, he saw only victims and suspects. Anyone young could be a victim, nearly any woman. And nearly any man could be the killer. Only the old were exempt.

Even the policemen he saw on the streets were potential suspects. The worlds of the police and the criminal were so close that there was always some seepage. And the criminals were drawn to the police just as the police were drawn to them. But only the police could check their own agents and their "non-staff assistants." What worried Kostoev was that it was more important for the police to keep certain of those agents and assistants in place and at work than to make them availa-

ble to the investigation. By now he was getting good information from the Rostov police. What concerned him was not its
accuracy but its completeness.

Sometimes when things were slow in Rostov, Kostoev
would ride the train to Shakhty instead of being driven there.
He would stare out the window at the landscape, flat steppe
interrupted by sudden stands of trees, mostly acacias, some
pine and birch, an occasional chestnut. But certain stretches
were familiar to him, and each one shone with the special
lugubrious glow of a murder site as it hove into view. If God was
just, thought Kostoev, He wouldn't let this go on forever.

Then a miracle occurred. It began with a vision, an appari-
tion. One night in August 1987 the headlights of vehicles crossing from the left bank of the Don to the city of Rostov suddenly
illuminated a young woman crawling on her hands and knees
alongside the road imploring help. Drivers slowed, then
stepped on the gas when they saw her blood-soaked face and
dress, fearing involvement. But when her red arm raised in
supplication was caught in the beams of a police car on patrol,
it pulled over and stopped.

Yandiev was woken at midnight by a call from the police. A
young woman had crawled out alive from a vicious rape and
attempted murder on the left bank of the Don, and was in the
Rostov Hospital. He immediately informed Kostoev, who was in
Moscow for the day and was electrified by the news. All past
disillusion was gone in a flash. They were alive again, inspired.

Yandiev went directly to the intensive care ward where the
woman, who had suffered twenty-one knife wounds—seventeen of which had penetrated her lungs—was lying unconscious. But the miracle continued. She regained consciousness
after a time, and the police artist Yandiev had summoned was
there by her bed, pencil and sketch pad at the ready. Yandiev
had a tape recorder in one hand as he leaned toward the
woman and began asking the questions that had to be asked.

Groaning, barely able to speak, the young woman kept drifting off into unconsciousness, the room suddenly so silent that they could almost hear the liquid dripping through the IV. Still, gently, deftly, Yandiev elicited details—what the assailant looked like, where they had met.

The artist did the best he could to render the woman's broken description into something that resembled an actual person, a man in his thirties with a mustache. The victim's and the police artist's rendition had apparently meshed into an accurate portrait for, by the time the picture went into distribution the next morning, one of the police had recognized the sketch as that of Misha Chumachenko, a former policeman who had been dismissed.

Further investigation revealed that Chumachenko was a known narcotics addict, and had been dismissed in connection with narcotics that had been seized by his wife, a detective, and which had then mysteriously vanished, causing her dismissal as well as his. A dishonorably discharged policeman fit the profile, and this time they had a witness who might stay alive long enough to identify him.

Chumachenko was brought in at once. He no longer had the mustache he'd had the day before. Chumachenko denied everything. So what if he shaved?—he had the right.

Yandiev's green eyes glowed as the idea of playing film director came into his mind. He ordered Chumachenko brought directly to a Rostov theater where a mustache was pasted back over his lip. Then two men of similar appearance—height, age, coloring, mustache—were rounded up. A number, 1, 2, or 3, was hung on each man. Then all three were videotaped individually while reading aloud a simple text written by Yandiev—"Let's go over to the left bank of the Don and get some shish kebab."

Yandiev raced back to the hospital with the videotapes, a monitor, and the cameraman. Thank God, the woman was still alive and conscious. The monitor was set up, the cameraman aimed his camera, ready to catch her reactions to the tape she was about to see.

"Take a good look at each of these three men," said Yandiev. "There's a number on each one. All you have to say is the number, that's all."

Man Number One recited his text. "Let's go over to the left bank of the Don and get some shish kebab."

The only sound from the young woman was that of air wheezing through the seventeen stab wounds in her lungs.

Two and Three played their parts on the flickering screen.

"Two," she said, closing her eyes. "Two."

Chumachenko was Number Two.

But the evening's performance wasn't over yet for Director Yandiev and his traveling crew. The next and last spectator was Chumachenko himself, who was under detention. Chumachenko watched the videotape with an intense, doomed silence, then said: "Alright, it was me."

Though entirely effective, the taping soon proved to have been unnecessary, for the woman, a strapping village lass by the name of Tanya, miraculously recovered and was able to identify her assailant in person.

Former police officer Chumachenko had fit the profile perfectly and had indeed attempted to murder this woman, even believing that he had succeeded. But none of the other coordinates matched up. He was not the killer being sought by Operation Forest Strip.

Yandiev had elicited a confession, but in subsequent interrogation sessions had never been satisfied with Chumachenko's explanation of his motive.

"Why did you try to kill Tanya?" asked Yandiev.

"She started asking if she could catch syphilis from me and I blew my top."

Yandiev didn't buy it for a second. It was clear that Chumachenko had attempted a copycat murder, to spite the police who had fired him and his wife.

Kostoev appreciated the methods Yandiev used to break the case and congratulated him on a swift and brilliant triumph, yet for both of them this victory too had the taste of failure at its core.

A month or so later, Kostoev and Yandiev pulled over to a roadside tavern on a warm evening. Some construction was being done out back, the workers, mostly Armenians, having just knocked off for the day. One of them was already enjoying the pleasures of the evening, pulling a young woman to himself and kissing her passionately. When the lovers' faces parted for a moment, Yandiev pulled Kostoev's sleeve and said: "Look, it's Tanya, back at it again."

It had been a miracle alright, just the wrong one.

D addy's home for a visit!'' shouted Kostoev's twin boys, which both warmed and broke his heart. The boys were growing faster than the weeping willow outside his room in the Hotel Rostov and he was missing it all. He was home in Moscow for the spring holidays beginning on May 1, May Day, and ending on May 8, Victory Day, that marked the taking of Berlin and the Soviet defeat of the Nazis.

Home was an aircraft-carrier-sized building with eleven entrances and fifteen floors. The district, on the northerly outskirts of Moscow, was known by the name of its subway station, Sviblovo, two stops from the end of the line. Home was two adjoining apartments, one with three rooms, the other with two, both equipped with kitchens, the bathtub and toilet in small separate rooms that were always side by side in such buildings. Home was his kitchen where he could drink tea at the table while talking with Asya who remained standing and working, both out of custom and of necessity. She respected the old ways and there was always plenty to do in a house with five children. They could talk, they could laugh, they both loved to laugh, hers high and gleeful, his Rabelaisian. Sometimes Asya would come bursting into a room laughing so hard she simply could not speak. Her falcon-faced beauty was in its full bloom, her chestnut hair was always covered; not only was

Islamic practice followed, but the colors she chose for her head wrap and dresses were of the vivid yellows, greens, and reds favored in the Caucasus and near Central Asia, though toned down in her choice by an architect's sensibility, which also required that the pattern be fine and exact.

She noticed that Issa was coughing, and coughing so hard his stomach shook and his eyes shut. And his hair was starting to thin, Issa who had sworn to her when they married that they would live in Moscow and he would be a general. That had made her laugh with delight at the time, but now it pained her that Issa had not been made a general yet, even after all he'd accomplished.

Asya had been reading books on medicine and nutrition, important things to know these days. She told Issa that she thought his hair must be thinning because of the vitamin deficiency he'd suffered during his youth in Kazakhstan. That would remind them of the exile they had shared and one of them would tell a story of those times and tears would come to their eyes in the kitchen in Sviblovo.

Home meant just lying around, watching television, doing a little reading. Glasnost meant there were new and interesting books about Stalin, the greatest killer of all time. Still, no one had yet explained the psychopathology behind that pipe and mustache, nor the man's phenomenal success.

Home was the dining room, the great room of the house, one of the long walls covered by a floor-to-ceiling wood and glass breakfront containing books and dishware. The opposite wall was hung with a flashing blue and red oriental rug in whose very center was an ornate black and silver dagger from Daghestan, of the sort carried by Shamil when he held out against the Russians for twenty years. Home was the long table in that room where he could carry on the best Ingush tradition—the women cook and set the table, the young men serve, and the older men eat, drink, and make merry when not discussing politics. And if Kostoev ordered his twin sons to dance a Georgian dance known as Lezginka, the only question they would ask was who should go first? The boys were very different. Amurkhan had his father's boisterous temperament, Zelimkhan his father's owlish gaze. While the men drummed on the table or clapped their hands, the boys would turn slow circles with a warrior's pride, then leap, twirl, fall to their knees, then leap back to their feet, lacking only sabers and black sheepskin caps.

On Victory Day veterans paraded through Moscow with all their medals, some of the older ones sitting on the benches in front of the Bolshoi Theatre listening to tapes of Soviet love songs of the early forties, fresh carnations in their hands, their eyes welling. Every so often a few of them would rise and dance again to that music.

Guests were an honor, a pleasure, guests made it a holiday. And if you had guests on a real holiday, as Kostoev did on Victory Day, then it was twice a holiday. The boys would have to dance longer and there'd be bottles of vodka in reserve, out cooling on the balcony, and close at hand.

After a long meal punctuated by elaborate toasts, some formal but heartfelt, others slyly jesting, Kostoev suddenly leaped to his feet and astonished his guests by throwing his cigarettes to the floor and declaring: "That's it! I quit!"

Spirits rose again in the spring of 1988, April's hope a fresh corpse. The body of a woman in her early twenties had been found in Krasny Sulin, a small town a little to the northwest of Shakhty. The corpse was naked, the head, neck, chest, and arms covered with blood. There were about ten small knife wounds in the neck area, but death had been caused by a blunt instrument. Part of her nose had been severed in what was estimated to have been four or five strokes. Her mouth had been packed with dirt.

As Kostoev looked down at the naked corpse, sometimes squatting down beside it, he knew that there was only one question worth thinking about. The temptation was to believe this was the work of their killer. That he wasn't dead or in prison or in a hospital or killing elsewhere. But that was a dangerous temptation, because Kostoev could not afford many more hopes mocking his team like mirages, sapping morale.

The murder had taken place near a train line, the local line that runs to Shakhty. That fit; but the handwriting of the wounds didn't. She hadn't been killed by stabbing or by strangulation, her head had been beaten in with some hard object, perhaps a hammer. It was true that their killer had murdered a mother and a daughter in one hour with a hammer. But the breasts of this victim had not been sliced or bitten off, nor had her abdomen been opened and her uterus removed. It was too soon to tell.

The first thing to do was establish the victim's identity. But nothing could be found. No one knew her. No one had reported her missing. The killer had taken her life and her identity.

Kostoev ordered intensive work to be maintained on learning anything about her, circulate her picture, recheck the missing persons' reports.

The Rostov Police were also checking closely on anyone who rented a garage, usually a small brick citadel against thieves, the steel front doors equipped with a two-pound padlock. Kostoev, however, never had much confidence in that line of pursuit and thought entirely too much effort was being put into checking drivers. There were tens of thousands of them. Better to put a few extra good men at the train stations, string them out along the local lines, the little out-of-the-way stations. The checking of motor vehicles lay outside the jurisdiction of both the police and the Attorney General's Office, belonging rather to the National Vehicles Registry, abbreviated in Russian as GAI. Normally, the principal function of the GAI is to wait alongside the road and halt vehicles that are in any way suspicious, to check the license and sobriety of the driver. There would of course be some in Rostov who would maintain that the GAI's actual function was simply to augment its men's incomes by the taking of bribes, a practice so well established that a rough understanding of rates had been established and a smart driver would know how much to slip the GAI man along with his license and registration. And, in fact, on the occasions when Kostoev went out and checked on the GAI's performance, he found the men much more occupied with lining their pockets than with driving infringements or the search for the killer.

It was maddening. Members of Kostoev's team had gone out to check police surveillance sites and found no one there. He could storm at the chief of police, but it was a waste of breath because no one was going to send his best men to hang around train stops, especially when the killer seemed to have ceased killing in Rostov Province. It had been two and a half years.

The Rostov police and Kostoev's group did get a computer that year, one that could both be fed all existing data and could run a specially created program that broke all murders down into four basic categories: Event, Victim, Crime, Analogues, before branching off into a root system of subcategories.

Kostoev admired science and technology, though he distrusted experts. Criminals were, initially at least, more inventive than detectives, and life always outstripped the mind. To catch murderers you need everything, computers and patience, autopsies and luck.

The information generated by the computer was sent to Valentina Saposhnikova, a leading specialist in biorhythms, whose institute was located in Leningrad. Given the patterns of the killings—time of day, day of the week, month, year, weather, place, blood type, all of it—when and where was he most likely to strike again?

Assuming of course that he ever did strike again. No, this one was not like Storozhenko, this one was unlike any others he had ever encountered. Kostoev had caught one murderer who'd bitten the genitals off little boys, but he had been a madman and not difficult to apprehend. This one was no madman. Sometimes this one did not even seem human at all, a specter rising out of Russia's blood-drenched soil, a Soviet vampire.

Soon enough it would be the end of June 1988 and, as he had done twice a year for the last two years, Kostoev would write his report containing statistics, successes, and protests, none of which could conceal the central fact that the case remained unsolved and he was therefore applying for another six months' extension.

But Kostoev remained confident that he would yet trap the killer, because confidence was both his natural sense of self and his basic approach to the world. Despair had to be fought as the enemy that led to self-betrayal.

Kostoev had consulted with computer programmers and a specialist in biorhythms. They both proved inconclusive, so why not a psychic? Kostoev had read that there was a team of psychics, two women and a man, with whom the Moscow police regularly consulted and who, supposedly possessing some strange sense of death's geography, were able to determine the location of a corpse. Not believing in it at all, Kostoev nevertheless went to see a woman in Rostov who had a reputation as a clairvoyant.

She told him that his mother was ill but not to worry, she wouldn't die, then added: "But what's the most important question you want to ask?"

Kostoev told her about the killer and asked where to find him, how to find him.

"It's not one killer," she said, "but two, a man and a woman. They cut out the organs and make some sort of medication out of them. They live on a mountain, very high up. The woman has been wanting to come to you and confess her crimes, she's even made some attempts to contact you."

The only benefit Kostoev derived from the session was that of additional doubt. He had never ruled out that the killer sometimes worked with someone else, quite possibly a woman. Women's clothing that did not belong to the victim had sometimes been found near the scene. And the presence of a woman could also help explain why children of good family might go off into the woods with strangers.

Russia always had its strange and hidden sects like the Khlysty who whipped themselves after orgies and the Skoptsy who castrated themselves to avoid sexual temptation. Such sects were known to still exist but had been driven even more deeply underground during the Stalinist years, and so were harder for him to find now. Sects that drank the blood of children and made potions out of human organs were also rumored to exist.

And it was not out of the question that the killer had found his soulmate, a woman every bit as depraved as he.

The clairvoyant had not told him anything he hadn't already suspected nor anything he had not already known. The image of the couple living high up on a mountain had no resonance for Kostoev, who was certain the killer lived somewhere in or around Rostov or Shakhty.

It had been almost three years since they'd had a kill that was unmistakably *his*. And that had been in August 1985, before Kostoev had even taken over the case. It was too long. That sort had to kill.

The longer the killer's silence, the greater became Kostoev's obsession with him. He would go to Aviators' Park, a place the killer had once favored, and sit there for hours thinking about the tall man with the briefcase and glasses. Maybe the killer's fury was spent. The textbooks were full of cases of people who had experienced a spontaneous remission of their vice. But this was more than vice and only death or prison could make that sort desist.

In 1988 it was Shakhty that provided the best lead and also the best laugh. Shakhty with its peasant huts, neat piles of coal, and gritty air became the hot spot for a while, pushing big, brawling Rostov into the background.

Word reached Kostoev that a lieutenant colonel working in the October Precinct of the Shakhty police had acted in a manner that was more than unbecoming. The lieutenant colonel, a strapping, bearded six-footer, was apparently a very violent man. As the information came in, Kostoev and Yandiev pieced the story together.

A representative of the Interior Ministry in Moscow had been in Shakhty to do an on-the-spot inspection. His duties fulfilled, he repaired with the lieutenant colonel to a food store whose manager had a special little room in the storage area where certain select people could relax after a hard day's work. Two women returning home late from a party saw a Volga car parked in front of the store and thought it might belong to the manager. He was a friend of theirs and would give them a lift the rest of the way home. To their surprise they found two strangers eating and drinking with the manager.

"It's not my car," he said, "but they'll give you a ride, just wait."

While the lieutenant colonel and the visiting official had eaten and drunk their fill, the women were seated in the back and the lieutenant colonel took the wheel of his Volga, driving the man from Moscow back to his hotel first. Then the woman who lived closest was taken home. Alone with one woman now, the lieutenant colonel detoured and slowed the car near some woods by a cemetery, not far from the train station.

"What are we doing here?" asked the woman in fright.

When the lieutenant colonel made his reasons obvious, the woman protested that she was married and wanted none of it.

Keeping one hand on the wheel, the lieutenant colonel struck her violently in the throat. In the ensuing commotion, she managed to jump from the moving car, breaking her knee in the fall. Still, she kept running. He pulled over and began running after her, but she reached the railroad station first.

When the lieutenant colonel saw that there were people there, he turned around and drove off. She screamed, the police came running.

What happened? they asked.

She told them.

What did he look like?

And when she told them, one of them could not help saying, It sounds like our lieutenant colonel.

She didn't think it possible at the time, but later learned that their lieutenant colonel was indeed her assailant, all the more reason not to bring charges against him. Even when Yandiev sought her out and brought her in to Kostoev for questioning, the woman still refused to bring charges. Time had passed, and she didn't want anything further to do with the lieutenant colonel.

But a case could not be brought against him unless charges were preferred. The only other possibility was the time-honored "parachute." It turned out that the lieutenant colonel could be proved to have been driving drunk when his car struck a woman, resulting in injury to her; in addition, he had falsified police papers to make it appear that his car had been stolen before the time of the accident.

Before pinning that parachute on him and dropping him into a cell for a few days, Kostoev decided to exploit the man's greed for women. A good-looking young woman spent a few hours in a hotel room with the lieutenant colonel, resulting in pleasure for him and a semen sample for Kostoev. It didn't match. But Kostoev called the lieutenant colonel in anyway and had a sample of his blood taken, at the same time letting him know that he could either perform his duties conscientiously in pursuit of the serial killer or go to jail for drunk driving and falsifying records.

The best laugh of the year concerned another member of the Shakhty police force, this one a captain. A homosexual waiter in a Shakhty restaurant was known to have a number of regulars on whom he performed fellatio. When pressure was applied, the waiter proved willing to name them all, a long list which included the police captain, a dignified man, on in years.

"We don't believe it. Not him."

"I swear to God," said the waiter. "There's no forgetting him, his sperm is so sour."

Kostoev and Yandiev would glow with suppressed laughter whenever "Captain Soursperm," as they now called him, happened to pass by.

Like all men on death row in Russia, Anatoly Slivko did not know the date of his execution and so always had reason to fear that any sound in the corridor, even the faintest, could be the guards coming for him. Relief would thus have been the natural reaction for Slivko when the guards informed him that he had a visitor, an important physician from Moscow, Dr. Kostoev by name.

Kostoev waited behind the desk in the interrogation room, well aware that he would have to be very careful with Slivko. Slivko could tell him a great deal; of all the killers their search of the prison system had turned up, Slivko was the most like the man they were seeking. Anatoly Slivko was a meek and mild-mannered man who seemed more at home in the company of children, company he frequently had had for he was both a teacher and a tour guide for youth groups. As a teacher he had won both official honors and the trust of his pupils.

To select individuals, always boys in their early teens, he would confide that he was making a film—everyone knew Slivko's great passion for photography—and he wanted the boy to act in it. The scene involved was that of a boy hanged by the Nazis in reprisal for partisan activity. All the boys Slivko asked were honored to participate and understood the need to keep their forthcoming participation secret, so as not to hurt the feelings of the boys who weren't asked.

Except that Slivko really hanged them. Photographing the

scene with a still camera, Slivko would neatly dismember the boys, separate torso from legs, feet from ankles. Never a suspect until caught in the act, Slivko had been sentenced to death.

With an air that was serious, authoritative, with just a touch of clinical distance, Dr. Kostoev, the "physician from Moscow," greeted Slivko and invited him to be seated.

The man Kostoev saw across from him was fifty years old with large light-blue eyes in a pale oval face. His hair was dark and his lips were thin.

"I'm interested in the way the criminal personality develops," said Kostoev with the assurance that he was stating nothing but the truth. "Any signs it gave in childhood, youth. But let's start with the physical, is there anything unusual about your body, your sexual organs?"

"No, my sexual organs are normal," answered Slivko.

"I'd like to see them," said Kostoev, who took a brief but professional look when Slivko complied.

"The only other thing I can think of," said Slivko, "is that I could never grow a full beard."

"If you would just remove your shirt for a minute."

Slivko removed his shirt, revealing a chest and arms that were entirely average except that his nipples were as long as a woman's.

"How did your nipples become so elongated?"

"My mother told me that when I was a baby and I was crying, she would massage my nipples and I would calm down at once."

"I'd like to ask you to write about yourself for us. How *you* see it, how it all looks to *you*," said Kostoev. "I'll come back in a couple of days, read what you wrote, and then there'll be some discussion sessions."

That was the sweetener. The physician from Moscow must be important enough to be given as many meetings as he needed with the prisoner. And that meant, for a while at least, the prisoner would not have to fear every shuffle in the hall-way.

What Kostoev knew, and could not let show for a second, was that Slivko was going to be executed very soon.

And so he had to be especially careful with every gesture and tone of voice. He didn't want a confession from Slivko, he wanted Slivko to hand him his very soul.

Slivko accepted the assignment, glad not only for the peace of mind it promised, but for the intellectual distraction. And part of him was a teacher, a good citizen who would have been mortified to appear before his students with liquor on his breath, as he would write. And the good citizen in him of course agreed that killers should be stopped. The problem always was that the killer in him was of a different opinion, and one more strongly held.

Two days later Kostoev was again driven the half hour of steppe and forest strip that separates Rostov and Novocher-kassk. This time he was accompanied by Major Burakov of the Rostov Police, who also had an interest in criminal psychology and would that day play the role of Dr. Kostoev's assistant, noting down his conversation with Slivko.

It was important that that conversation go as well as possi-ble, for now Kostoev knew that two or three hours after it was over, Slivko would be executed.

Though he had never witnessed an execution, Kostoev knew how they were done. The prisoner was taken from his cell, brought to a place which screams could not penetrate, forced to his knees, read his sentence, and executed with a shot behind the right ear from a nine-millimeter Makarov ser-vice pistol.

The identity of the people who performed the executions was one of the police's most closely guarded secrets. And Kostoev had to battle long and hard to force them to divulge those names. People who volunteer to kill are necessarily inter-esting. They were all checked out "operatively," the records scanned to establish their whereabouts on given days, and all eliminated. Now, in a few hours one of them would pierce Slivko's brain with "nine grams," the bullet's weight becoming its nickname.

They pulled into Novocherkassk, long the capital of the Don Cossacks, with its tree-lined streets, solid, sometimes elegant yellow brick homes. When, after defeating Napoleon, the Cossacks had marched into Paris in 1814, their leader had been so impressed with the city that, upon his return, he ordered an arc de triomphe built in Novocherkassk as well as a great cathedral from which boulevards radiated in a star-like pattern.

Kostoev had given Slivko a green elementary school notebook with the multiplication tables on the back cover. Now Slivko returned it, every page filled with neat handwriting that had clearly come after serious thought.

Kostoev began reading it at once. Slivko wrote that when he was twenty-three, he saw a car accident in which a boy in his early teens had been killed. The boy was wearing the uniform of the Pioneers, a communist youth organization, white shirt, red scarf, and black shoes. There was a lot of blood and flaming gas on the street. Slivko was both horrorstruck and fascinated—for he had seen a vision of his true beloved.

Seeking to save himself from this "sweet nightmare," Slivko married, only to be immediately disgraced by being unable to break his wife's hymen on their wedding night; a surgical procedure was later required. Though sex with his wife filled Slivko with "nausea, despair, and tears," he did manage to father a son. For a time, being the father of a newborn child gave him the courage to fight against the terrible fantasies that pounded on him until he at last surrendered, becoming, as he put it, a "slave of fantasy."

All Slivko's victims were boys in their early teens, the principal recipient of his lust their shiny black shoes. Though the red scarf of the Pioneers was part of his fetish, he should not, he wrote, "be suspected of any fascism here in the least."

The part of Slivko's mind that made judgments continued to function. He condemned himself for sinking so low as to fantasize about his own son. "I could write about what I did in two very different tones. In one I would stigmatize, but in the other I would extoll sadism as something elevated and beyond the reach of ordinary people . . ."

In speaking of his character in general, Slivko said that he did not smoke, drink, or swear, and had a deep love for nature. "Which brings one to the not very consoling conclusion that even an outwardly respectable person can harbor evil."

Completing his quick but careful read, Kostoev said: "We'll discuss this more after I've had a chance to sit down with it, though I would like to ask some questions now. Did you ever go back to the scene?"

"I always had the desire to. And I would go back, a few times, usually a month afterwards, sometimes earlier," replied Slivko, who went on to admit that the photographs he took of his victims and later developed in his own darkroom were only sufficient to satisfy him for a month or so. He also pointed out that he had never before said anything about his fantasies about his own son but now, aware that he had no hope, had decided to write the full truth.

"And did you kiss your victims?"

"Yes, when they were unconscious."

"Next time, we'll talk in greater detail," said Kostoev, with a brisk nod, bestowing the mercy of illusion.

CHAPTER 13

It was the year of the four tantalizing corpses.

On March 9, 1989, a man who went about collecting bottles to eke out a living found three bundles wrapped in clothing and tied with twine in a pipe that was part of Shakhty's drainage system. He needed only to open one package before going to the police. They notified the leader of Kostoev's group in Shakhty, who in turn notified headquarters in Rostov.

The body of a young woman had been dismembered into three parts—head, torso, legs from the hip down. The autopsy indicated that the body, about two weeks old, had decayed sufficiently as to make a precise determination of the cause of death impossible. Strangulation was, however, the most likely cause. Damage had been done to the young woman's vagina and uterus. Her upper lip and nose had been severed and placed in her stomach. Her blood had a high alcohol content. A piece of newspaper—the January 6, 1989, edition of *Pravda*, printed in the Ukrainian city of Kharkov—was found stuck to the left side of her torso.

Her identity was quickly established. Tatyana Ryzhova, sixteen years old, runaway, drifter, living the fast life.

Some of the "handwriting" looked the same, but the older the corpse the harder to read. And there was one crucial difference. Their man did not dismember. The body had been dismembered, packed, then brought by some means to the drainpipe. One old man recalled helping a man pull a child's sled over the railroad tracks but it was dark and he couldn't remember what the man looked like. He did seem to recall there were some bundles on the sled.

And their man did not like to work indoors, he always needed his woods.

But it was winter and hard to work in the woods. Maybe he lured the woman back to an apartment? Would he risk the screams? Or would he make sure there were none?

There were many strong signs that it was their killer—the type of victim, the type of wounds. But the corpse was so decayed as almost to be illegible. That, plus the fact that the woman had been killed in a dwelling and had, uncharacteristically, been dismembered prevented Kostoev from feeling anything more than a hunch.

The investigation would be pursued energetically and, based on past experience, chances were that they'd solve the murder, they'd solved something like seventy so far, it just wouldn't be the man they wanted.

Still, even if there were only the slightest chance that the killer was back on his old grounds, all extra measures possible had to be taken. If the killer was now so driven that he was operating even in the winter, everything must be done to entice him. It was time to use decoys.

One evening at the end of the workday, Inspector Kostoev decided to stroll over to Rostov's Main Railroad Station and check up on the implementation of those instructions.

Dim brown, ill-lit, vast, the train station echoed with announcements, buzzed with destinies and destinations. Cab drivers cut through the crowds looking for suckers to take on the scenic route. Barefooted Gypsy women begged for kopecks, a dirty child asleep in one arm, the other extended. Soldiers in khaki, sailors in blue. Stranded families sleeping on benches. The bright, hard faces of prostitutes, plying their trade a little more freely now than in the old days, when some of them would chalk their price on the bottom of their shoe and flash it to potential customers.

Then Kostoev spotted a woman who was not only good-looking, well-dressed, but all too familiar.

She recognized him too as he began walking over.

"You're on duty?" asked Kostoev.

"Yes."

"Undercover?"

"Yes."

"Decoys?"

"That's right."

"Then what are you all dolled up for?"

"What do you want us to do," she asked with offended pride, "wear dirty skirts and lie around on benches?"

"Exactly!"

"What if people we know see us?"

And it was no better with the teenage boys who had been enlisted to serve as decoys, in theory always under the watch of a plainclothesman. A tough-looking boy with a dirty face and a black eye caught Kostoev's attention. He seemed to be just hanging around. Usually boys that age hung out in groups, but still there were loners at every age.

After watching him for a time, Kostoev sidled over to the boy and said: "What are you doing here?"

With proud confidentiality, the boy replied: "I'm working with the police, Burakov's team, I'm stationed here."

The next morning at a meeting with the police, Kostoev exploded. "Better no decoys than decoys like that. The killer isn't interested in well-dressed women. And what if that boy had said to the killer the same thing he'd said to me! No more decoys for now."

The second body of the year was found by four teenage boys who were tramping through the woods near a rural sta-

tion called "Leskhoz," meaning "Tree Farm." The station consisted of two concrete slabs about thirty yards long on either
side of the tracks, the far side possessing a simple structure in
which passengers could take refuge from bad weather. There
were a few huts clustered by the tracks in one of which the
stationmaster lived and sold tickets. Other than that it was
essentially a wooded area favored by hikers and mushroom
gatherers.

Though the body was very decayed, it was easy to identify
because the victim's internal passport had not been taken. It
was quickly determined that sixteen-year-old Evgeny Muratov
had traveled to Rostov almost a year ago in July 1988, to make
application to the Railroad Institute, attend a soccer match,
spend the night with his aunt, and return home the next day,
even having told his mother he would be on the 4 or 7 P.M. train.
Ten months had elapsed since the boy was killed when his
body was found on April 10, 1989.

The handwriting was similar, many knife wounds, no less
than thirty, and the complete removal of the genitals. Train
tracks, trees. But the boy was of good family, not a street kid.
And besides, it was almost a year ago and the trail would be as
cold as the ground in the woods.

On May 8, 1989, the Soviet Union celebrated its victory over
Hitler and Kostoev his over cigarettes, for it had been a year to
the day since he had astonished his guests by hurling a pack
to the floor and swearing an oath at the table. Red Square
resounded with the cheers that grew less vociferous and assured with each passing year. Standing on the mausoleum that
contained the mummy of Lenin in a coffin of glass—one of
Stalin's ideas that Lenin's widow had resisted strenuously but
unsuccessfully—Mikhail Gorbachev waved to the passing
throng. The veterans gathered in the little park in front of the
Bolshoi Theatre, jaunty again in uniforms and medals, tangoes
playing on scratchy tapes.

There was a lot to discuss with his friends at the table. The country was changing quickly now and no one knew where those changes were leading. But if in fact there was going to be something like justice on the political level, there could be some hope of the Ingush regaining the territories Stalin had taken away from them before packing them off to the mines in cattle cars.

The Ingush lands were now divided almost in two. The lowland meadows and the mountain valleys were connected by a thin strip of road controlled by their enemy, the Ossetians, a passageway Kostoev referred to as their own "Danzig corridor." It still seemed impossible that the lands would ever be reunited, but it was a time of swift and dazzling change, Andrei Sakharov had gone from exile to Congress in a matter of months.

The only thing that wasn't moving swiftly was the hunt for their killer. Not that speed was the issue. They rolled along solving crime after crime, a threshing machine that took everything in sight. His two conversations with Slivko on death row had given Kostoev more insight into the mind of the psychopathic killer, but he knew he was chasing a different sort of man. His was big and strong and full of a fury that the quiet Slivko with his pale oval face and large light-blue eyes had never felt.

His was more complicated than Slivko, who had only one sort of victim, boys in clean white shirts, red scarves, and shiny shoes. His killer killed boys and girls and women, and exhibited none of Slivko's fetishism. All his ritual was in the act itself.

The most disheartening thing Slivko had said was that monsters like him gave no outward sign. He was the last one anyone would have suspected. It still could be anybody.

Then the holidays were over, beautiful as a prisoner's dream. The worst thing about returning to Rostov was the hotel, the lack of hot food. At least this time Kostoev would have a new weapon for that front, an aluminum electric frying pan that he managed to locate in Moscow.

Spring and early summer are sweet in the south of Russia. Though the sun turns the spring mud almost immediately into fine golden dust, the breezes that lifted that dust from the ground were still mild, more refreshing than abrasive. The sky was deepening to a royal summer blue but the sun had not yet become a tyrant. Melons appeared in the market. Still tentative, Rostov resumed its pleasures along the Don.

On July 14, remains were discovered in a park in Rostov. The name on a nearby notebook was that of Alexander Dyakonov, a nine-year-old boy who had not returned home from second grade on May 11. Once again the advanced state of decay made certainty impossible, but the probable cause of death was blows to the head with a stone, though the many knife wounds had also contributed. There were shallow wounds in the upper chest and throat area that had not been inflicted to kill. The boy's tongue and genitals had been removed.

Now there were three. And that carried some weight in itself. But all three were alike in their decay and their inconclusiveness. None of them rang the chord of certainty in Kostoev.

What he needed was a fresh corpse and a fresh trail.

They were combing deeper and deeper all the time. One of the few women on Kostoev's team, Nina Petrovna, of whom he always said that she had the "body of a woman but the soul of a detective," had almost exhausted the seemingly inexhaustible files of Rostov province's mental hospitals. They had even checked out the executioners in the prison system. And the cavalcade of perverts had never ceased, but had now lost its garish allure.

Inspector Yandiev, diligent, driven, was tracking people who had been reported missing as long as nine years ago. Two young men had gone from Rostov to Ukraine, but only one had returned. The other was reported missing. Later, his passport had been found in Rostov and turned over to the police. Working with Vorobinsky, one of the people on the Rostov police Yandiev considered truly competent and dedicated, they decided the case was worth looking into.

They called in the young man who had returned alone from that trip to Ukraine. Now, nine years later, he was in his early thirties, married, working, a good citizen. He categorically denied any knowledge of what had happened to his traveling companion. The other young man had simply chosen to remain in Ukraine while he had come back home to Rostov.

Enlarging the circle of contacts and using his conversational gifts, Yandiev learned that the young man had not been a model citizen nine years before. Yandiev called him back in for questioning.

"There's a statute of limitations even on murder," said Yandiev, "and it applies if a person has not committed any other crimes in the meantime. Your record's clean for the last nine years, all you have to do is tell us what happened."

The young man resisted all Yandiev's approaches and gambits, until finally, in a rush of sobs and emotion, he revealed the truth that had tormented him every day for nearly ten years.

"We went to Ukraine to gather poppy seeds to make heroin, to use and to sell. We ground the seeds in meat grinders. We filled three sacks, that's a lot, it'd be worth a million rubles today.

"I said to him—'That's enough, let's go.'

"He said—'Let's grind up some more and put it in our knapsacks.'

"So we went back to grinding seeds. All of a sudden I feel something and I turn around there he is coming at me with a knife. We fought, I got the knife away from him and killed him before he could kill me. Then right away I took him out to the woods, dug a grave with the knife, and buried him. I threw all the poppies away and went back to Rostov. And I've lived with that every day of my life. Now it's over, thank God, it's over."

Yandiev's lips curled with a smile of ironic compassion, the compassion for the young man, the irony for himself, for he had just solved the wrong case again.

Yandiev traveled to Ukraine with the young man who showed him where the body had been buried. Yandiev went directly to the local police and inquired whether a body had ever been found in that spot. One had, but no murder investigation had been launched.

"And what did you think," said Yandiev, "that the man had buried himself?"

The golden sun of August rolled above the endless steppe of southern Russia, the shade of every leaf now prized like cold water. On the sixth of the month Issa Kostoev turned forty-five.

Some of his group had lost hope, but not Kostoev. If the man was alive, he would find him. If God was just, He would not let this go on forever. Now more than ever this was the watchword of Kostoev's faith.

Time had only deepened his fascination with this uncanny killer. He could think of almost nothing else. The killer was his first thought upon rising and his last as he fell asleep in Room 339 of the Hotel Rostov.

In Slivko's death-row interview he had said that he constantly desired to return to the scene. He had in fact returned when the photographs he had taken lost the flavor of reality and when only the actual place itself could bring memory alive.

A closer watch was now being kept on the Tree Farm train station and on the park in Rostov where bodies had been found that year. The drainpipe in Shakhty where the first corpse was stumbled upon by the man collecting bottles was not watched as closely. Woods and parks held the romance of murder, that exalted passion beyond the reach of ordinary people, as Slivko had put it. But a drainpipe was just a convenient disposal site.

The walls of Kostoev's office were covered with maps of Rostov Province, diagrams, aerial photographs which he studied for hours on end while waiting for the phone to ring with electrifying news.

All the train and bus stops which the killer was thought to have stalked before were now under surveillance by teams of two plainclothesmen. Sooner or later he had to return to Shakhty or Rostov, sooner or later he had to return to his favorite haunts, if he hadn't returned already.

Then, in the midst of everything, Kostoev had to solve the case of the missing detective.

One day he stopped by Inspector Lukyanonok's office to ask him a question.

"He left about fifteen minutes ago," said one of the men who worked with him.

That was unfortunate. Lukyanonok was an experienced man and Kostoev wanted his opinion on something. Lukyanonok had joined the team late in the game. In fact, he was already preparing for his retirement, having accepted a tough post in the frozen far north because the pay was higher there and an inspector's pension was figured on his average income during his last five years. To Lukyanonok's surprise, he found that he had been transferred to a group run by an inspector who was by nationality an Ingush. Lukyanonok had begun his career in the justice system in the mid-forties and he had known many Ingush "special resettlees" in Kirghizia, to which republic some had been shipped. Like few others, he was able to appreciate the steepness of Kostoev's rise.

Kostoev in turn respected him because he was an older man and knew his business, which was why Kostoev had dropped by to ask him a question. Maybe he could catch Lukyanonok in the hotel that night.

Over 200 Justice Department investigators had already worked on the case. Kostoev found most of them worthless. That wasn't surprising, no one was going to send away their best men for six months, a year. It was the perfect chance to get rid of some deadwood. And unless Kostoev indicated an inspector by name when requesting by telegram "qualified inspectors who have investigated murders," he would have to take the luck of the draw.

And those who were assigned to him did not wish to remain long in Rostov either. It meant living in a hotel, far from their families, their children. It meant working on a case which did not at all seem destined to shower them with glory, raises, promotions, stories about them in the national press, their picture in a newspaper, magazine, maybe even on television.

Kostoev had observed in the hotel how natural little groups formed, "communes" they called them, three or four or five people who gravitated to each other, felt at ease with each other, and naturally divided up the errands of life, one shopped, one cooked, one found the vodka. And the little groups did commerce among themselves, borrowing and lending. Kostoev himself would let people use his aluminum electric frying pan, or might ask for some sugar since he liked two or three lumps per cup of tea.

For one reason or another Kostoev forgot to drop by Lukyanonok's room that night, and only thought of it again the next afternoon.

"Where's Lukyanonok?"

"Haven't seen him all day."

That was odd. Lukyanonok was a portly man nearing retirement age who had not so far exhibited any great tendency to go chasing about in pursuit of the killer.

But Kostoev was not taking any simple answers the third time he stopped by Lukyanonok's office and found him gone.

"I want to know where the hell Lukyanonok is."

"No one knows. He's missing."

Kostoev did not quite believe that no one knew, but he wasn't about to start interrogating his own men. That's not what they were there for. But he did dispatch a party to search for Lukyanonok. Anything could have happened. They returned late that evening with no further word, but would be on it again the next morning.

They were spared the effort. Inspector Lukyanonok, looking both exhausted and mildly jubilant, himself turned up the next morning at Kostoev's door.

"I've got it!" announced Lukyanonov.

"Got what?" said Kostoev.

"You didn't know?"

"Didn't know what?"

"Oh, so then you didn't know," said Lukyanonok, all jubilation gone. "Alright, alright, I'll tell you what happened. I'd had a few drinks, maybe more than a few, I went back to my room to fry up a little canned food in that pan of yours, and I must have closed my eyes for a little while because the next thing I knew someone was pounding like crazy on my door and the room was full of smoke.

"Well, to make a long story short, the frying pan had melted and set the rug and curtains on fire, and I would have slept through the whole thing if the floor concierge hadn't seen the smoke coming out from the door. And that's where I was the last three days."

"Where?"

"Running around the whole province of Rostov trying to find another electric frying pan for you."

"You spent three days looking for a frying pan when we're supposed to be looking for a killer?" asked Kostoev with a great laugh of amazement.

"I felt so bad about it."

But all the jokes wore thin quickly, nerves were starting to fray, even Yandiev, normally so even-tempered and self-possessed, lost his composure and would have physically attacked the Rostov detective if he had not been restrained.

"You're from Rostov, the killer is killing your children, I tell you twice to turn in a written report and twice you show up with no report!"

They seemed to have gotten the break they so desperately needed when the fourth corpse of the year showed up on September 2, 1989, in a forest strip near a rural bus line. Like all the previous three, the body was in a state of decay so advanced that the cause of death could not be precisely determined. The victim's identity was, however, quickly established as Elena Varga, nineteen, a citizen of Hungary studying animal husbandry in Novocherkassk, a student, not a drifter. Still, all the other signs of the killer's handwriting were present—breast, uterus, and nose with upper lip removed by knife. The body had been found naked and covered with leaves, an act that seemed both to conceal and memorialize.

It might have been the wounds on Varga's body, it might have been the location, a forest strip, that began strengthening Kostoev's inclination to believe that the killer was back.

Two deep cuts had been discovered in a tree about thirty yards from the body. Had the killer made them? When? Why? Was there still some fury in him even after what he had done to that young woman? That portion of the tree was sawed out and brought in as material evidence, though there was little chance of matching the knife marks on the tree and on the body which, since the end of August, had been exposed to the elements for two weeks.

Or perhaps it was the single gray hair found on the victim's skirt that finally edged Kostoev across the line of doubt. On September 6, 1989, four days after the discovery of the fourth corpse of the year, Kostoev made the case of Elena Varga an official part of Operation Forest Strip.

Kostoev winced at the little boy's innocence. "And while the man was beating my bottom with the switch I looked around and saw him making peepee in his pants."

Several children had been brought in to Kostoev for questioning. All of them had told their parents that a man who worked for the railroad had caught them playing near the tracks or throwing stones at trains and had made them take down their pants so he could whip them for a punishment. Some got thirty lashes, some fifty, some a hundred.

Even against his own better judgment, Kostoev felt a flash of hope again. From the very start the profile had specified that the killer might travel in connection with his employment, and one place to look for him was among the workers of the railroad system.

Since Yandiev had been working in the transportation system when Kostoev requested he be assigned to his team, Yandiev was the perfect person to head the hunt for the railroad sadist. But something told Kostoev that he too should get personally involved in this one. He began taking children as decoys into the woods near the train line that ran near the Botanical Gardens at the outskirts of Rostov, where several children had been whipped.

Kostoev spent hours with the children by the tracks, watching them play, watching the trains go past, rushing like the days and weeks.

But the railroad sadist was not attracted by the bait.

Maybe he had gotten wind of the hunt? That was another similarity he shared with their killer, he could vanish just as suddenly into silence.

And then he proved himself arrogant, beating a young boy when the hunt was at full heat. But once again he eluded detection, and once again lapsed into inactivity, having gotten what he wanted.

Yandiev was always tenacious, but now had to be especially so—Kostoev had assigned him to find the suspect who operated in Yandiev's own area of specialty, transportation. And there was nothing worse than failing at what you were supposed to be best at.

Legwork and seemingly casual conversation paid off for Yandiev again—some of the railroad workers thought there might be something a little odd about one of the track inspectors, a big strapping man of around fifty, unmarried, aloof. Yandiev brought him in and he was identified by the children he had beaten.

Kostoev interrogated the man, but no great application of his art was required to obtain a confession.

"I've got a problem, a problem," the man said. "The only thing that gives me sexual pleasure is beating children's bare bottoms."

But, he insisted with the ease of the innocent, he had nothing to do with the killings. His blood was checked, he was given a batch of the copious pornography they had confiscated in their raids, so he could provide a sample of his semen. The types didn't match, and he had solid alibis for all the days on which killings had occurred. He was just another criminal whose indictment had to be written and sent on to the courts.

Another case solved, another hope extinguished.

It was already late December. Storm clouds filled the vast steppe sky from Siberia to Rostov. The first snows of the year were falling, people were wearing fur caps, some even had the earlaps down. Soon Kostoev would have to write the end-of-year report and request the next extension. He had arrived in Rostov to head the investigation in November of 1985, and it was now late December 1989. More than four years, longer than World War Two!

CHAPTER 14

E ven Kostoev couldn't bear the sight. But he remained squatting beside the body of the boy on last year's leaves. The boy was almost naked, his pants at one ankle. It was their killer, no question about it. No one else could inflict such hateful wounds. And now the killer was even crueller than before. Not only had he tormented the boy with knife pricks on his throat and chest, not only had he inflicted wounds after death—easy enough to detect, for wounds inflicted after death barely bleed—not only had he taken the genitals and wounded the eyes, this time he had opened the body and ripped out the heart and intestines with his bare hands.

It was the section of lower intestine beside the body that seemed most horrible to Kostoev, but it was also what gave him an idea. Since there would almost definitely be semen in that section of lower intestine, was the killer, by removing it, making it more difficult for them to determine the type of the semen?

Unable to bear it any longer, Kostoev rose and walked away. Yandiev and the others continued their inspection of the site, but there was little to be found. The body had been discovered by a man walking his dog in the Botanical Gardens and, by the time Kostoev, his men, and the police had arrived, the area had been trampled by curiosity seekers alerted by word of mouth.

It was a morning in early March 1990, a chill drizzle softening the ground to first mud.

Kostoev hated himself for not having caught the killer. He felt guilty of this murder. And yet for all his pains of conscience and self-contempt, Kostoev also felt delivered, inspired, by the certainty that the killer was back in Rostov.

Now Kostoev realized that another boy killed in Shakhty at the beginning of the year had also been a victim of their killer. That body had been found after more than a month, and decay had raised doubts. Now those doubts were dispelled. And the four corpses of the previous year could now be seen in a different light. The killer might have been back for as much as a year.

Kostoev returned to the body where the photographers were just finishing with their melancholy art. He exchanged glances with Yandiev, whose green eyes were lit with the same certainty as Kostoev's.

"There's a name on the waistband of the pants," someone said.

"Check everyone who works in this park, everyone who walks his dog here, everyone who lives in the area, every house, every member of every family, every school, every missing persons report, the nearest train station, the Main terminal, everything!" Kostoev ordered.

Returning to headquarters, Kostoev checked with the night duty man as to whether any crimes or unusual incidents had been reported.

"Many people called in and said they'd sighted UFOs over the Botanical Gardens," the duty officer told him.

"Are you serious?" said Kostoev.

"They were all written down," he said, pointing at the ledger.

For a second, Kostoev thought he had been wrong to picture the killer as a demon from the old-fashioned world of folklore; this killer could be from another planet doing the kind of research on people that people do on animals. But that was only a momentary reflection, a measure of the uncanniness of it all. No, it was a human being, if that was the word for him, who had killed that boy in the Botanical Gardens.

People were really working now, really "gnawing the ground," as they called it. Everyone wanted the killer now, for the glory and the promotions and to be done with the goddamned thing.

The boy was identified almost immediately as Yaroslav Makarov, an eleven-year-old with the habit of skipping school and going to the train station where he bummed money and cigarettes. Yaroslav was of good enough family—his father was an engineer, a tall man whose white goatee made him look like a figure from the nineteenth century. His mother was an engineer as well, fleshier than her husband and more emotional. The father identified his boy.

Not only were the investigators able immediately to establish the victim's identity, this time they found three witnesses. But the resulting composite sketches were all very different. The first witness was an amazingly spry and clear-eyed woman in her middle seventies who had volunteered to work in the Botanical Gardens and who quite literally ran from one task to the next. The perfect Russian she spoke seemed that of the old aristocracy. The woman had seen a tall, slope-shouldered man with glasses who was carrying a briefcase. The man had been aware of her and had even turned in her direction and glared at her to deflect her attention. And, yes, she would be able to recognize him if she saw him again.

The Botanical Gardens contain a great variety of trees, nearly all of which are numbered and labeled with their names in both Russian and Latin, all trees being venerated in the treeless steppe. The park also contains a spring whose waters are said to have restorative powers. Near where the spring bubbled out of the ground and began quickly winding through the trees to join the other waters already running over the rocks, a Georgian, while cupping clear water in his hands, had noticed someone he considered odd, suspicious. The Georgian too was able to furnish a description that could be used to make a composite sketch; within days they arrested a cobbler with a large collection of very sharp knives. But his blood type was wrong, he had alibis for the most recent killing and all the others. After his release the cobbler, who had a history of mental illness, began calling Kostoev three times a day with leads, suspects, ideas. It took more effort to get rid of him than to find him in the first place.

A few witnesses had seen Yaroslav Makarov at the Main Train Station on the day he was killed, and all reported him in the company of a bearded man in his late twenties who was wearing a black and yellow striped jacket.

"I want everyone in Rostov with a beard brought in!" ordered Kostoev.

Thousands of Rostov's bearded suddenly found themselves politely but firmly requested to accompany a plainclothesman to headquarters. Bearded men grew afraid to leave their homes. If they went out they could be stopped every four or five blocks by a different team and brought into a different station, no matter how loudly they protested that they had just been checked. Kostoev was forced to initiate a receipt system so that the honest bearded men of Rostov could go about their business.

Finally, the right bearded man was found, a twenty-eight-year-old Moldavian wearing the requisite black and yellow jacket.

"Yes, I talked to the boy at the station, he kept asking for cigarettes and spare change, but I didn't kill him."

"We have a witness who says she saw you leave the train station with the boy and head toward the Botanical Gardens," said Kostoev.

"She's lying."

"We'll see."

Kostoev ordered that two bearded men similar to the Moldavian in appearance be brought in for a lineup. The lineup was set up in the usual fashion, the three bearded men, dressed alike, seated on chairs, two witnesses observing that the law is obeyed, the inspector at his desk. The witness came in, a woman in her middle thirties. Her slovenly clothes and heavy makeup displeased Kostoev.

"That's him," she said, pointing at the Moldavian, taking only long enough to look once closely at each of the three.

"She's lying!" insisted the Moldavian.

"Are you sure?" Kostoev asked the witness.

"I'm sure."

Kostoev frowned and found himself more inclined to believe the bearded Moldavian.

Later that day Kostoev dropped by the apartment where the witness lived. It turned out to be a communal apartment, one family per room, shared kitchen, shared toilet, the sort of situation where people either come to value or to loathe each other.

All the witness's neighbors loathed her. "The bitch will screw anyone and she informs on people to the police."

That was all he needed to hear. Back at the police station, Kostoev asked the chief if the woman in question was one of their paid agents.

The chief replied: "How am I supposed to know all our agents, we've got hundreds?"

"But you can find out."

The chief picked up the phone and made a few calls while Kostoev waited.

"She works for Vlasov," said the chief.

"And who found this witness?" asked Kostoev.

"Vlasov."

After that, it didn't take long to establish that Vlasov had brought in one of his agents as a witness to make himself look good. He had had to provide her with a good, detailed description of the bearded Moldavian because the woman had never even been at the train station that night.

It only reminded Kostoev that no matter how hard some of the police were working, he was, in the end, at the mercy of the men on patrol at train stations and parks, usually country boys, the word "professionalism" not even in their vocabulary.

Kostoev and his team had come up empty-handed, a crazy cobbler, a bearded Moldavian. It would have been dispiriting except for the sure and invigorating knowledge that their killer was alive and active again.

That certainty reached even into dreams. Shortly after Yandiev had examined the body in the Botanical Gardens, he dreamed that the woman who lived with the killer came to see him.

"I've something to tell you," she said.

"What?"

"I was there with him at two or three of the murders."

"Which ones?"

"Come with me and I'll show you," she said.

They went to a peasant hut thatched with straw near a forest strip. There were bodies stacked up like cordwood behind the hut.

"Why didn't you come to me earlier?" said Yandiev.

"Now that the police are hunting him everywhere, he's at his wits' end, and he's started looking funny at me."

"Where is he now?"

"At work."

Yandiev watched from a distance as the man was led handcuffed through a doorway. He could only see him in outline, tall and slope-shouldered. The man was coming closer. Any second now Yandiev would see the features of his face, any second.

* * *

In the spring of 1990, after the killing in the Botanical Gardens, the killer lapsed into one of his periodic silences. Kostoev was not surprised. The man would have to step carefully now that he had returned to his favorite places, Shakhty and Rostov, after at least three years away.

Kostoev sensed that it was late in the game. And something had changed. The killer, a "masterful player," had returned to the places where he was most actively sought. Why? Was he so jaded now that he needed the extra thrill of playing the most dangerous game, challenging Kostoev directly?

Spring became summer and still no word. The mud dried to yellow dust, the narrow beaches on the left bank of the Don filled with people, though some preferred to get out of town entirely, heading for the coast of the Black Sea in Georgia. The Cossacks who lived in Rostov returned for a time to their settlements by the Don River, which is very broad, slow, and quiet south of the city. Reeds grow thick along the Don and out of its waters as well, some extending six feet to form small passageways for boats. The Cossacks fishing the river see nothing but reeds and water, except when they drift past a larger settlement where the red and green cupolas of a cathedral hinge steppe and sky.

Kostoev too longed for some rest. In mid-August he traveled the relatively short distance from Rostov to his summer home in Ingushetia. The high brick wall and immense wooden gate lent the interior the feel of a compound. Baby chicks ran freely in the high grass, roses bloomed at the foot of an evergreen. The house, which his father had built on his return from exile, was also made of brick, a large and serious dwelling with an ornamented tin roof.

There was pain as well as pleasure in going home. Kostoev was reminded how little time he'd had with the children. It was not only how quickly they were growing, but how quickly they were becoming contemporary, modern, in a way he could neither fathom nor quite approve. And any trip to the mountains to see the old towers, silver-bearded men arranging a prayer rug on a mountain peak, the air fresh with the hiss of rushing rivers, also meant a trip through Ossetian territory on the "Danzig corridor" which only reopened wounds that went back to Stalin.

Still, home was the place where he could have the unimaginable luxury of falling asleep outside after a good lunch and a few vodkas, the children, heads cropped close for summer, stifling their laughter at Kostoev's mighty snores.

The three-day idyll ended on August 17 when Yandiev called. The killer had struck again. An eleven-year-old boy had been found in the high reeds near a public beach in the town of Novocherkassk. His father, a police officer, fainted when he saw his son.

It was quickly determined that the murder had taken place three days before, on August 14. Making use of the media liberated by glasnost, Kostoev appealed for anyone who was on the beach on the day of the murder to come in for questioning. A few people remembered seeing a tall man with a briefcase, not dressed for the beach, who kept walking back and forth as if waiting for someone, or looking for someone.

One week later, on August 24, the skeletal remains of a woman were found in the woods near the Tree Farm railway station, actually an outlying stop, two long strips of concrete by the tracks, a few huts in one of which the stationmasters lived and sold tickets. The victim was naked and covered with leaves, branches, and a few scraps of *Izvestiya,* the newspaper of the Soviet government. An autopsy revealed that she had been killed in April or May. Efforts to identify her failed to make any progress.

The killer had operated there before, back in 1988. Every single stop on this line would now have to be watched at all times by plainclothesmen working in pairs. And the Botanical Gardens would have to be patrolled by men wearing park workers' overalls.

The number and chronology of the 1990 murders had to be readjusted in late September when the body of another boy was found in the Botanical Gardens. The body had clearly been there at least two months, which meant that the killer had struck in late July. Now it was clear that he had killed in January, March, April or May, late July, and mid-August. It was going to be another major series.

The remains found in the Botanical Gardens were those of Victor Petrov, age fourteen. He had disappeared from the Central Bus Terminal in Rostov on July 28. Anxious about missing an early morning bus, his mother had taken him and his two brothers to the station to spend the night there, sleeping on benches in the huge upstairs waiting room. Around one-thirty in the morning Victor asked his mother for ten kopecks to go down and buy himself some mineral water. That was the last his mother saw of him. She was, however, able to add one important detail—there had been a tall, slope-shouldered man, wearing glasses, near the dispenser; she'd seen him make change for a few people.

Kostoev found it impossible to sit still. His nerves were taut and it had been more than two years since he had had the solace of cigarettes. He walked the streets and parks, day and night. Late one evening, he saw a woman jogging down a dark tree-lined path.

"You should run where it's light," said Kostoev.

"What goddamn business is it of yours?" she retorted.

"When your cervix is on the pavement it'll be my goddamned business!"

Then everything changed on October 30 when the body of a sixteen-year-old boy was found in the woods near Tree Farm station. But this time, what mattered was not the place nor the killer's "handwriting." What mattered was the pile of neatly folded clothes, the victim's, which had appeared on a trail in the woods a day or so after the killing. The locals swore they had not seen them before. And a day later they reported that a red rag had now been tied to a tree.

Kostoev took it personally. A taunt from his prey—it takes you two weeks to even find a body, perhaps I can help. It was a mocking laugh, a slap in the face, or rather a hair held up to your face.

But Kostoev also wondered: Were these actions part of some signal system the killer was using to determine if the body had been found, if a place was still safe?

The game was being played differently now. Kostoev would play differently too.

Having to fight not only the Rostov police but the trend of the times for full disclosure of crime in the press, Kostoev nevertheless won his battle for a news blackout. The killer must have no idea of what they knew. Kostoev even ordered his team to treat the current phase of their investigation with secrecy. He had never ruled out the possibility that the killer had connections with local law enforcement.

Nineteen ninety's seventh victim, handsome, athletic, blond, sixteen-year-old Victor Tishchenko, was found on November 3, only three days after he was killed. This time too the killer placed the boy's jacket by the side of the tracks, where it could not fail to attract attention. Standing in the freezing rain on that November day, Kostoev said aloud, half vow, half matter-of-fact: "This time I'll get him."

Eight days later, on November 11, Yandiev, working with Major Ivan Vorobinsky of the Rostov Police, found two witnesses, young women, medical students, who had seen a man on the local commuter train reducing a young boy to tears while trying to get the boy to go somewhere with him. The boy's mother must have been expecting him, because the man kept saying, "I know your mother. Get off with me here for a while, then I'll take you right to your mother."

"Have you seen the man since?"

"Yes, he rides the trains often," one of the medical students told them.

"And you could identify him?"

"Yes."

Kostoev questioned them on November 12. He asked if they would be willing to ride the trains the next day, accompanied by plainclothesmen. The medical students agreed to report to Kostoev's headquarters in the early afternoon of the next day, November 13.

Shortly before the med students were due to arrive, the phone rang. Another corpse. Tree Farm station. A woman.

A hard cold rain pounded the corpse and all the men in hats and coats standing around it, their breath visible in the air.

This time everyone was there, the heads of the police, and Kostoev's top men.

Kostoev exploded: "How could this have happened! This is one of the places that's supposed to be watched!"

"Our people were at their posts," answered the chief of police. "They were taking down names. Some people were here gathering mushrooms, there was even one man we'd checked out a few years back."

"What's his name?"

"I don't remember his name, but the report's on file."

Kostoev had to read the latest report in a district police station, for it had not been forwarded to Rostov.

The report stated that on November 6, 1990, at approximately 1:15 P.M. a plainclothesman, Igor Rybakov, on patrol at Tree Farm station noticed a suspicious person. The man cleaned his shoes at the little pump near the stationmaster's house before crossing the tracks to the passenger shelter. Rybakov found something too hearty about the way the man greeted three mushroom hunters who had taken refuge from the cold drizzle. The man was tall with gray hair and carried a dark blue over-the-shoulder bag, one strap of which had broken and been tied in a knot. The bag was partially open and appeared to contain a change of clothing. The man had a bandaged finger, fresh scratches on his hands and right earlobe. Leaves and twigs were stuck to the back of his jacket.

Rybakov identified himself and asked the man to present his documents. He made a note of the name in his notebook—Andrei Chikatilo.

Rybakov's superior had come to the Tree Farm station later that day and Rybakov reported to him verbally, adding that he would have detained the man but was afraid to since he was alone, his partner having failed to show up. The fact that the report had never made its way to Burakov's central card file indicated to Kostoev that it had been telephoned in and rejected as unnecessary; the suspect had already been checked out, a point he confirmed later.

Andrei Chikatilo had indeed been checked out before, in 1984, in connection with a murder in Shakhty. Though it was late and still raining hard, Kostoev went at once to police headquarters in Shakhty where he requested the 1984 file on Andrei Chikatilo. It was not a large file because the suspect had not proved of interest and, in addition, there had been a warrant out for his arrest for the theft of socialist property, some linoleum, a battery. But what there was to read only made Kostoev want to read more.

When being questioned, Chikatilo had admitted to suffering from "sexual weakness," the same term they had used in their profile, the same term Slivko had used when speaking of himself. He had admitted to sexually molesting several children, which resulted in his dismissal as a teacher, the same profession as Slivko's. And some of the information on his work history pointed in the right direction, especially his taking new employment in Rostov in August 1984, just when the murders began to reach new peaks.

The next morning Kostoev telephoned Major Burakov, the police officer in charge of the central card file in Rostov.

"Do you remember this Chikatilo?"

"Sounds familiar."

"As an exception to the rule, I would like to see anything on Chikatilo in the for-police-use-only files."

As he read, Kostoev was increasingly shocked and encouraged. Shocked because even under the rules of police procedure, a great deal of this material should have been turned over to him. Encouraged because everything he read about Chikatilo seemed like the next page in the life story of his killer. Most fascinating of all was the arresting officers' description of Chikatilo stalking from train to terminal. Not to mention the fact that when the police did detain him, he was carrying a sharp knife, rope, and a jar of Vaseline in his bag.

But his blood had proved to be Type A; the killer was known to have semen Type AB.

That was the hard objective fact at the core of it all. Or was it? Labs make mistakes all the time.

And there was some recent research that had established the existence of "paradoxical secretions": In some exceedingly rare cases certain men may have blood and semen that are of different groups or, under certain conditions, approach boundaries close enough to seem different.

Yandiev had accompanied Kostoev to Rostov police headquarters and there proceeded to xerox the pertinent pages, with or without the police's permission. Kostoev did not ask. Kostoev's own inspectors could put a finer point on many details, and would begin doing so immediately. Exact dates were necessary.

Things were starting to get specific.

He entrusted the most important information gathering to Nina Petrovna, instructing her to ask only for the list of all those who had taken business trips in Chikatilo's various workplaces during a given month. Chikatilo's name must never be mentioned.

There was no question that Chikatilo should be tailed. The

KGB were masters of invisible surveillance but, administratively, it would be very difficult to have them assigned that task, not impossible, but definitely time-consuming. And that was bound to meet with resistance from the Rostov Police, who would insist that they were the ones who were supposed to provide surveillance.

But there were two great problems in relying on the Rostov Police for surveillance. If Chikatilo got the slightest whiff of them, he could leap in front of a speeding streetcar or slip away somewhere and hang himself. Kostoev could not help feeling that there might be a few people on the Rostov police force who just might prefer that.

The parameters began lining up the next day. All the information assembled by Nina Petrovna and others on Kostoev's team regarding Chikatilo's business trips clearly demonstrated that he could have been in each of the places where murders occurred on the day they occurred. So, on November 17, Kostoev instructed the Rostov police to place Chikatilo under close surveillance.

Those were heavy, overcast November days, snow falling, sleet underfoot.

Kostoev could not wait very long in the hope of catching Chikatilo in the act. Sooner or later he would have to arrest Chikatilo; now the most important task was to devise a strategy for interrogation that grew out of everything he knew about the man and the case. In the end, it was probably going to be the two of them alone in a room.

Back in Room 339 of the Hotel Rostov, Kostoev stared at a small photograph of Andrei Chikatilo, obtained from the personnel department of one factory where he had worked. The man had dark, dilated pupils ringed by gray, eyes that seemed to look past you.

One thing was absolutely clear—the usual approach, that confession mitigates a sentence, was completely out of the question here.

Now Chikatilo was followed from the time he left his apartment in Novocherkassk in the morning to take a commuter train to the factory in Rostov where he worked, until he was home and the lights were turned out. He was leading the life he had been leading all those years, wearing brown and gray clothes, carrying a blue bag over his shoulder, buying newspapers at the kiosk, back home in time for dinner.

Chikatilo showed a penchant for striking up conversations with children and adolescents, but he would break them off if any adult so much as approached. However, judging by the old police report and the current surveillance, Chikatilo was constantly on the hunt, always looking for the weakest stray, the safest chance.

It was another fitful night for Kostoev. He had begun to fear the very thing he had hoped for from the surveillance—catching Chikatilo in the act. Something told him that Chikatilo would not emerge alive from the confusion, that he would somehow take his own life or be shot down by an overzealous cop.

Kostoev knew that if there was to be any hard proof against Chikatilo, it would most likely be found in Chikatilo's own apartment, or in one of the several he had access to. But those apartments could not be searched until Chikatilo was arrested. And, not having any hard evidence on Chikatilo, how could he arrest him?

Kostoev did have enough evidence to place Chikatilo under arrest for the ten days the law allowed for the interrogation of a suspect. But if he failed to obtain a confession, Chikatilo would have to be released and, again, by law, could not be rearrested for the same crime. A chancy business.

On the night of November 18 Kostoev made his decision, in fact, two decisions, that would take a day of paperwork to implement. Surveillance would have another two days to catch Chikatilo in the act.

Without yet informing the Rostov police of his intentions,

the following morning Kostoev petitioned the Attorney General of Rostov Province to issue a warrant for the arrest of Andrei Chikatilo, effective November 20, 1990. He also wrote a request to the head of Rostov Province's KGB, General Major Kuznetsov, stating:

"Considering the nature of the crimes under investigation, as well as the personality of the suspect, Andrei Chikatilo, I hereby request your permission that Andrei Chikatilo be held in the KGB's isolation prison in Rostov.

"For your information, the arrest and detention of Andrei Chikatilo is planned for November 20."

Then suddenly it was November 20, and Andrei Chikatilo was in a room full of cameramen, police, typists, removing his shirt as the police physician had instructed him. Noticing that Chikatilo had the same kind of elongated nipples as Slivko, Kostoev immediately ordered: "A closeup of his chest!"

The photographer took a few quick steps forward, the flash commanded by Kostoev dazzling Chikatilo for an instant.

After a brief, formal questioning, Chikatilo complained of heart pains and requested that interrogation be put off until the next day, a request Kostoev was glad to grant. He wanted Chikatilo alone and the police chief's office was full of people. Kostoev had been able to order Chikatilo's arrest because, after three days alone in his hotel room, he had realized how to crack Chikatilo—by offering him the one thing he deserved least in the world, compassion.

PART IV

C H A P T E R   1 5

Inspector Kostoev signed for the prisoner in Room 211. "Hello, Andrei Romanovich."

Chikatilo remained silent.

"Why don't you say hello, Andrei Romanovich?"

Still no reply.

"Listen to me, Andrei Romanovich, I'm an inspector performing his duty and you're a man under arrest. Since we have to work together, we should treat each other with respect."

"Hello," said Chikatilo very quietly.

"You may be seated," replied Kostoev, glad for the first small victory of the day.

He watched Chikatilo move to the chair with a slow, elderly gait which said, How can you be doing this to a person my age?

It was almost four o'clock in the afternoon. Kostoev had not wanted to begin the interrogation until he knew what the search of Chikatilo's apartment had produced. That was their last chance for material evidence, bloody clothing, a body part. But his home proved as clean as his crime sites.

Twenty-three knives, some police newspapers, no real evidence.

"And how are you feeling today, Andrei Romanovich? Yesterday you said you had heart pains. That's passed now, I don't need to call a doctor?"

"No," said Chikatilo.

Kostoev worded his question so that a yes or no answer would suffice. It didn't matter in the least what Chikatilo said, as long as they stayed in contact.

Chikatilo was phlegmatic, very cool, indifferent. Difficult to communicate with, difficult to excite.

"Here's what I think we should do," said Kostoev. "First, let's just talk, then we can do an official interrogation, in the presence of a lawyer if you like."

Chikatilo didn't answer but Kostoev could see that he still had his attention. The conversation was important to Chikatilo too, who had to determine what sort of case they had against him.

"You do understand why you have been arrested?"

"They arrested me in 1984," said Chikatilo wearily. "And for the same crimes."

"Have you heard of me?" asked Kostoev.

"No, I haven't."

"You read the papers, do you remember in the middle eighties when an inspector from Moscow came to Rostov and arrested seventy people in the justice system?"

"I read about it."

"Well, I'm that inspector. And you must also have been aware that a special team from Moscow has been hunting you. In all of Russia there are nine or ten Inspectors of Crimes of Special Importance, and I'm their chief. And I'm the one running your case. So, don't think for a single second that this is going to be 1984 all over again, the usual quick once-over. Your case was investigated by the highest agency in Russia. And that investigation has now led to your arrest."

Chikatilo kept his head inclined, his eyes averted so that Kostoev saw more flesh than feature in the face. But he could tell that Chikatilo was weighing every word.

"In 1984 you were in a holding cell. Do you know where you are now?"

"Yes," said Chikatilo, "the KGB."

"That's right, the place where the most important criminals are held, spies, corrupt officials. You're being interrogated by the head of Crimes of Special Importance in a KGB isolation prison, you're an intelligent man, Andrei Romanovich, you should be able to draw the proper conclusion."

Chikatilo retained his pose of silent attention.

Kostoev paused to allow the point to sink in and to watch for any reaction from Chikatilo. But there was none. His hands were folded, his legs were crossed.

It was then that Kostoev smelled it for the first time, an odor unlike anything he had ever encountered. He could not even think what to compare it to.

The odor was as hideous as it was unique, and it threw Kostoev for a second, almost causing him to gag. Chikatilo was wearing a fresh pair of black overalls, which meant that the odor had to be coming directly from him.

"Under the law," said Kostoev, overcoming his revulsion, "you have the right to remain silent. But remember one thing—I'm not a crazy man. I've been an inspector for twenty-seven years and I wouldn't have risked arresting you if I didn't have the evidence in hand."

Kostoev paused again to underline his point with a silence that quickly filled the room, bare except for the T-shaped desk, the wooden safe, the portrait of Dzerzhinsky, founder of the KGB.

"And here's my last remark on that subject, Andrei Romanovich," continued Kostoev. "You must have heard that a number of people were arrested in Rostov in connection with the murders. And those people confessed. I had those people released.

"So, just ask yourself, Andrei Romanovich, if I would release people who confessed to the murders, would I arrest someone without sufficient grounds?

"I have all the evidence I need to convict you. But there are many things I don't understand at all. I don't understand why those murders were committed, what the motive was, what made you do it. I can't believe a sane man would be capable of such crimes. And under our law the insane are not imprisoned or executed, but hospitalized and treated."

Kostoev had taken his position, and his tone, and this time when he paused it was because he was through.

If Chikatilo felt trapped by Kostoev's logic into which only a single exit had been built, it was too soon to tell. In any case, it was time to get down to specifics.

"I'm ready to begin questioning you officially, Andrei Romanovich, would you like your lawyer brought in?"

Chikatilo nodded. The lawyer was brought in. By law the formal interrogation had to begin with the basic questions—name, place and date of birth, nationality, party member or not, place of employment. Kostoev again stated for the record that Chikatilo was being held as a suspect in the murder, on sexual grounds, of thirty-six women and children.

"Would you care to make a statement about the charges that led to your arrest?" asked Kostoev.

"I consider the suspicions against me to be mistaken," said Chikatilo, his voice quiet but clear. "I haven't committed any crimes. I was arrested six years ago and charged with similar crimes. Both then and now I was arrested illegally since I have committed no crimes. I think I am being persecuted by law enforcement because I have written to several governmental agencies to complain about the illegal actions taken by the town leaders of Shakhty who have allowed people to construct a garage in the courtyard of the building where my son lives."

Chikatilo had now made his opening move. Not only was he not guilty, he was himself the victim of injustice. Double denial.

But the most important thing was that Chikatilo was willing to discuss the issue. That kept the game going.

"Precisely when, where, and under what circumstances did you injure the middle finger of your right hand?"

"I received the injury about a month ago at the factory where I work, to be more precise, at the loading dock. I was moving some crates of spare parts for a pickup. But the truck didn't come for them until a few days later. I didn't tell anyone that I had injured my finger while moving crates and there wasn't anybody there when it happened. Wait a minute, later on I did mention it when I was back in my department at the factory. Why no one else was there on the platform and why I didn't go to the doctor right away, I couldn't say."

Judging by the wound, the nail missing, the area puffy and green with iodine, the injury had been inflicted, as Chikatilo said, about a month ago. But it hadn't been done by any crate. Probably his next-to-last victim, Tishchenko, a big, strong boy who would have put up a good fight, had inflicted that wound.

Kostoev became aware of the odor again, and still couldn't think what to compare it to. It wasn't from the injured finger.

"But why were you, a senior engineer, lugging crates around, especially when the truck hadn't even arrived?" asked Kostoev.

"I simply wanted everything ready well in advance."

"Have you had any injuries on your face in the last ten to fifteen days, and, if so, under what circumstances did you acquire them?"

"I haven't had any scrapes or abrasions on my face in the last two weeks. No, that's not true, I did get a scratch on my right ear from a bush on Berdichev Street while on my way to work."

Chikatilo spoke as if he were wearied by the necessity to fight against the most extravagant of interpretations being put on the most banal of events.

But it was clear to Kostoev that Chikatilo's tired voice was like his pitiable, elderly shuffle—only a move. Every word, every silence, every inflection and gesture was a move and only a move in that bare room.

Kostoev knew that Chikatilo, however deranged he was in

some ways, had still remained perfectly logical in others. He had eluded capture for years, done his job, lived his life, taken his little granddaughter out for walks.

The logic of survival dictated that if Chikatilo accepted that Kostoev possessed sufficient evidence to indict him, he had also to accept that his only hope was to be found legally insane. But Kostoev also knew that if he were in Chikatilo's position, the one thing he would try to do was determine precisely what evidence the investigator did possess.

That placed Kostoev in a bind. He had to keep his few hard facts and witnesses in reserve, otherwise he'd be left with nothing at the end. But some of those facts, presented as questions of forceful assurance, had to be used early on in the interrogation, so that Chikatilo would realize the weight and range of Kostoev's evidence. It was time for one of those questions.

"Can you tell me where you were and what you were doing on November 6 and 7, 1990?" asked Kostoev.

Everyone would remember where they'd been on the 7th, it was Revolution Day.

"Yes, I know what I did on those days," said Chikatilo. "On November 6, I was at work until lunch, actually until four o'clock. I wasn't working in Rostov that day but at our plant in Novocherkassk. After work, I walked home and I was home with my wife that evening. On the morning of November 7, 1990, my wife and I took the 7:50 local train to Rodionovka where my sister, Tatyana, lives. We stayed with her until the 9th. I wasn't anyplace on those days."

Chikatilo's lie gladdened Kostoev's soul. It would not even matter now if Chikatilo suddenly changed his mind and said—wait, yes, I remember now . . . All Kostoev wanted was that first reaction, guilt's automatic tropism against truth.

"Were you at the Tree Farm train station on the sixth of November?"

"No," said Chikatilo. "Not on November 6, nor at any other

time have I been at the Tree Farm station. I've never had any business there."

"When you were arrested, your internal passport was taken from you. Tell me, had you given your passport to anyone recently?"

"No," said Chikatilo, "I didn't give my passport to anyone recently."

"I can show you a statement made by police officer Ryba-kov to the effect that on November 6, 1990, at approximately two o'clock in the afternoon, you came out of the wooded area near Tree Farm station, and that at the time you had injuries on your hands and face. How do you respond to Patrolman Ryba-kov's statement?"

"I was not at the Tree Farm station. And I don't know why he says I was."

Kostoev paused to give Chikatilo time to remember that last murder, the rain, the woods. Time to remember that his identity had of course been checked at Tree Farm station on November 6. And time finally to realize that he and Kostoev were now united by the knowledge of those lies.

"That's enough for today, Andrei Romanovich," said Kos-toev.

CHAPTER 16

I want to warn you about something, Andrei Romanovich," said Kostoev on the second day of interrogation, November 22. "When I see that you are being evasive, I have to say to myself, no, this man is just a clever criminal trying to avoid punishment like he did in 1984. It's one of two things—either you're a clever criminal or you're a person with obsessions you can't control. I wouldn't expect a person like that to lie to me if I asked if he were at such and such a place. So, don't lie to me, Andrei Romanovich, when I ask you if you were at Tree Farm Station on November 6."

Chikatilo did not reply or respond. His strength was in his passivity. But passivity was also a receptive state. Kostoev could reinforce his message, that resistance was useless, even harmful. It would deprive Chikatilo of the only hope he had—a hospital as opposed to a bullet in the brain.

"There must have been all sorts of contributing factors in your childhood that will have to be examined. And I'm sure that there will be many institutes interested in studying you, for you are, after all, a very rare phenomenon, Andrei Romanovich."

Suddenly, Kostoev had the feeling that he was alone in the room. Chikatilo's gray eyes were glassily vacant, a cavernous silence where the person had been.

Kostoev had never quite seen anything like it. He had watched men withdraw into themselves when they were on the verge of confessing, to take a final counsel with themselves. But concentrated as they were, Kostoev would still have the feeling that they were there in the room, the personality having vanished but not the person.

After a few minutes of fascination, Kostoev spoke again: "Andrei Romanovich, I'm talking to you. I know that everything you do is an attempt to avoid the truth, but it's too late for that. You kept the truth about yourself a secret for a long time, but your secret is out now. And this silence now is just another attempt to avoid doing what has to be done. And what has to be done is for you to confess to all the crimes you have committed."

But then Kostoev saw that it was useless and himself fell silent.

There was nothing he could do but peer at Chikatilo crouched in his chair, hands on his lap. The finger of the right hand was still bandaged. A hand bitten by a boy fighting for his life, a hand that tore children's insides out for enjoyment.

That reminded Kostoev that he had to be on guard every second. He could no more betray the slightest hint of his hatred for Chikatilo than he could betray his paucity of hard evidence.

Chikatilo's silvery aura began to return to him, his eyes were no longer so dull a gray. And the odor was back.

"We were discussing the need to make a full confession," said Kostoev when he saw that Chikatilo's attention had returned.

"I would like to write a statement to the Attorney General," said Chikatilo.

Kostoev gave him pen and paper, remaining in the room as Chikatilo wrote.

Kostoev did not expect much from this, hardly a full confession. But what mattered was that he had moved Chikatilo off the dead point of absolute denial which had a natural, magnetic pull for any criminal.

Chikatilo wrote quickly, in bursts, his handwriting fine, jumpy, seismographic. When he was done, he signed the statement and handed it to Kostoev.

"On November 20, 1990 I was arrested and have been in custody since that time. I want to be honest about the way I feel. I am in a state of deep depression, I admit that I have committed certain acts and that I have deranged sexual feelings. I sought psychiatric help before because of headaches, loss of memory, insomnia, sexual disorders. But the treatments given me or devised by me brought no results. I have a wife, two children, I have a sexual weakness, impotence. People laughed at me because I couldn't remember anything. I wasn't aware that I touched my genitals frequently, and was only told so later. I feel humiliated. People ridicule me at work and in other situations. I have felt degraded since childhood and have always been in pain. In my schooldays I was swollen from hunger and went around in rags. Everybody jeered at me. I studied so hard in school that I would sometimes lose consciousness and faint. I am a university graduate. I wanted to prove my worth in work and gave it my all. People valued me but then suddenly management would take advantage of my weak character and force me to leave without any reason. And that happened many times. I complained to higher authorities, exhausting myself in the process. And I was fired in disgrace. And that happened many times. Now that I'm older the sexual side of things is not so important to me, my problems are all mental. Once again I have worn myself ragged writing complaints to Moscow about those swine who allowed my son's house to be blocked up by the construction of an outdoor toilet and private garages.

"And how much of this is my responsibility? In perverted sexual acts I experienced a kind of fury, a sense of being without restraint. I could not control my actions. I have felt inadequate as a man and a person ever since childhood. What I did was not for sexual pleasure, rather, it brought me some peace of mind and soul for long periods of time. Especially after viewing all sorts of sexual videotapes. What I did, I did after watching videos of perverted sex acts, cruelties, horrors."

Kostoev was surprised at how deep a crack he'd made. Chikatilo was not yet able to call his acts by name, referring to them as "what I did." But he was no longer denying his crimes in the least, he had begun to explain, to excuse.

Chikatilo's new position was clear. He had accepted the "exit" of mental illness, referring to his having sought psychiatric help in the very opening of the statement. And now having taken that position, Chikatilo had to insist that he had not been driven by a search for sexual pleasure but by obsessions that were beyond his control.

Chikatilo presented his life as one of unjust insult, unjust failure. That was good too. He was justifying, not denying. The crack was there, now it needed to be wedged open.

"And now, Andrei Romanovich, it's time for you to tell me about your first murder."

"I'm not feeling that well right now," said Chikatilo. "I'd like to put that off until tomorrow."

More than satisfied with the day's results, Kostoev agreed. Besides, he understood—even Chikatilo found his crimes unspeakable.

CHAPTER 17

And how are you feeling today, Andrei Romanovich?" asked Kostoev, extending his hand to Chikatilo, who hesitated for a second before extending his.

It was a risk, Kostoev knew, because fingers could transmit inadvertent impulses. The handshake had to bind Chikatilo closer to him, to win trust.

Chikatilo must see him as his only hope on earth, and as someone deeply interested in him as no one had ever been before. Chikatilo must also see him as a fool who could be made to believe that Chikatilo did not torment children for sport and pleasure, but because he was driven by some violation of his own soul that went all the way back to childhood and birth.

Chikatilo did not answer Kostoev's question as to how he felt, but only nodded to indicate there were no problems and to thank him for asking.

When Chikatilo was seated, Kostoev resumed his place at his desk. Chikatilo still had not looked at him once. That had already come up often in the interrogations being conducted by the other investigators who were talking with Chikatilo's family and coworkers. He never looked anyone in the eye, even his wife. And that deprived Kostoev of his most powerful weapon—his unwavering gaze which challenged the other's eyes to stay with his, their courage proving their honesty. He could keep his gaze on Chikatilo so that Chikatilo would be constantly aware of it, but that was not as good as looking directly into his eyes.

"You know, Andrei Romanovich," said Kostoev, his voice easy with intimacy and rich with confidence, "I was looking through the list of your victims after you left yesterday. And I had to say to myself, not as inspector of course but just as a person—most of these people were the scum of the earth, drifters, sluts, retards. And I'm wondering how you saw those people."

"Déclassé elements," said Chikatilo with a slight, silent laugh that showed his upper teeth. Kostoev noticed how short the upper teeth had been worn, usually it was the lower. Kostoev smiled a little too at Chikatilo's use of a Marxist term.

"Was it easy to strike up a conversation with that sort of people?"

"It wasn't difficult," said Chikatilo, pausing to wonder if he was admitting something he shouldn't. "They're always pestering people for one thing or another, money, food, cigarettes, something to drink.

"I traveled a lot in connection with business. I was always at train stations and terminals. I'd see them there all the time, they'd start drinking in the morning. And they always had money to buy shish kebab from the stands, I never had that kind of money."

Kostoev could hear the tone of injury in Chikatilo's voice, a man offended by all life's ugly injustice.

"And so you were often in those kinds of situations," said Kostoev to keep the conversation going.

"Very often. I traveled all over the Soviet Union. I saw bums and drifters everywhere I went. Fighting all the time, bothering children. And I'd watch them going off into the bushes, and I knew why they were going there. And that would only remind me of my own sexual inadequacy. And I'd ask myself if that sort of scum even had the right to exist."

Now at last Kostoev had the feeling that Chikatilo the murderer was beginning to speak directly to him.

"Those drifters," continued Chikatilo, "used to go off into the woods near the stations. Bodies were found in the woods near train tracks. There were stories in the papers and people were always talking about it."

Chikatilo could bring himself to say no more. Kostoev saw that he was gingerly broaching the subject of corpses in the woods, but still wasn't ready to put himself into the picture.

Chikatilo was speaking the way he had written yesterday, jerkily, in bursts. That too might be an attempt to appear disordered in mind, or it might be the hysterical panic that precedes confession, when the suspect is still struggling against the impulse to be free of his secrets.

"To save time today, Andrei Romanovich, why don't we eat right here in the office," proposed Kostoev.

Bread, sausage, and kefir to drink were brought to them there in 211.

It was difficult for Kostoev to eat with that odor still in the room. And after glimpsing Chikatilo's upper teeth that day. But Kostoev had to will himself to appear at ease, the only hope for justice was in his playing his part to the hilt.

Chikatilo's own appetite was, Kostoev noticed, healthy to say the least. He chewed his sausage greedily and gulped his kefir.

The guards who observed Chikatilo through the peephole in his cell door had reported to Kostoev that Chikatilo had been masturbating behind a newspaper. Dreaming, no doubt, about pleasures past.

Kostoev could not detect an ounce of contrition in Chikatilo, not really surprising, since contrition was simply compassion after the fact, and Chikatilo had demonstrated none in, as he put it, what he'd done.

After lunch, Chikatilo resumed his complaint. "They constantly poisoned the atmosphere at work for me. I consider myself a normal person, professionally speaking. But they would always fire me at the first chance they got. And everyone would laugh at me because I suffered from such a terrible memory that I always had to carry pen and paper to write everything down right away so I wouldn't forget it."

That, of course, was something that could be checked out at work, but it was also interesting that Chikatilo made a point of it. Proving what? That he suffered memory lapses? That his mind was so disordered that it could not perform the most ordinary functions?

But the information Kostoev was receiving from the other investigators indicated that Andrei Romanovich was quite well organized, especially when it came to his own private affairs. It turned out that throughout the years when he was murdering Chaikatilo always had access to an apartment and recently had even falsely certified that he had divorced his wife, so that the state would allocate him an apartment of his own.

That was a little odd since the only person whose opinion seemed to matter to Chikatilo was that of his wife, Fenya. He worried about what she thought of him now and about what would happen to her. It was a sore spot for him. It might also have been the reason Chikatilo had not been able to remember what year he had been married when Kostoev asked him that question on the day of the arrest.

"I am trying to help your wife and children," said Kostoev, deciding to touch that sore spot again, and, as well, by using the word "trying" to let Chikatilo know that nothing definite yet had been arranged. A lot still depended on him.

"How is Fenya?" asked Chikatilo, hesitantly.

"She's fine, and so are the children."

"I would have been alright if I'd just stayed home with Fenya."

Kostoev nodded understandingly though he knew this man

would have gone on killing until the end of his days if he hadn't been caught.

"And I had terrible problems with my son's apartment," said Chikatilo, his voice for once achieving some timbre of feeling. "The director of the music school in Shakhty and some of his cohorts decided to build an outdoor toilet and private garages in the courtyard where my son lives. This would have blocked all his windows. For me that was an intolerable injustice and I began writing letters of complaint. I wrote to the Party Committee, the Executive Committee, I even wrote to President Gorbachev. The whole thing drove me to my wits' end. And that, along with my impotence, not that it matters so much anymore, and my arthritis and all the insults I have suffered drove me more than once to the brink of suicide," said Chikatilo, bursting into tears.

Kostoev understood those tears. Those were not the tears of contrition, nor were they even tears of self-pity. This was just the physics of a psyche splitting open, as something long withheld was suddenly being released, as natural as sawdust flying from a piece of sawn wood.

"Go ahead, cry, get it all out," said Kostoev warmly and with no hint of derision. "It's good for the soul."

When Chikatilo was done weeping, he looked up and said, "I'm exhausted now. Have my lawyer here on Monday and I will give you a detailed, accurate statement of my crimes."

Kostoev hesitated for a moment. The prisoner was promising to confess in detail on Monday but in exchange was asking for the weekend to prepare himself. But Kostoev had ten calendar days to obtain a confession, Saturday and Sunday would count as two, leaving him only five. A quick glance at Chikatilo still wiping his eyes decided the question.

"Until Monday then, Andrei Romanovich," said Kostoev, noticing, with slight distress, that Chikatilo had now abandoned his elderly shuffle and left the room almost briskly.

CHAPTER 18

Inspector Kostoev knew that he had made a serious error even before Chikatilo was brought in on Monday morning.

He had received a disturbing report from the KGB isolation prison's supervisory staff. On Sunday, one of the guards, making a periodic check on Chikatilo through the surveillance aperture in the cell door, had observed the prisoner wrap his glasses in a towel, then break them.

It was an absurd act, one that could have no practical significance. Chikatilo had worn his glasses to a few of the sessions last week. A new pair of glasses could be found in ten minutes.

The act might have been pointless, but it was not meaningless. It was clearly an expression of defiance, the sign of a decision to cease cooperating. Chikatilo had not been able to resist the initial onslaught, but the weekend had given him time to assess the damage and marshal his forces in a new strategy.

Chikatilo was brought in, accompanied by his defense counsel, Attorney Miloserdov.

Kostoev saw that Chikatilo had a more confident air today but looked a touch shamefaced as well. He still would not meet Kostoev's eyes. And that was a victory for Kostoev, one that had to diminish Chikatilo's confidence by some amount. The only way to test Chikatilo's confidence was to clash with it.

Kostoev greeted his prisoner with fatherly irony.

"On November 23," began Kostoev, "you stated that on November 26 you would give detailed and accurate testimony about your crimes. Do you wish to give that testimony during this interrogation?"

"I have not committed any crimes," said Chikatilo. "I did in fact take local trains often but I didn't commit any murders. On November 23 I did in fact in my own hand write that today, November 26, I would give testimony about my crimes. No one forced me to write that, still, today I declare that there is nothing for me to testify about. I have committed no crimes."

Kostoev's expression was somewhere between a laugh and a frown, indicating to Chikatilo that he had never heard anything so ridiculous. Had Chikatilo suddenly forgotten the most basic facts—that he was in a KGB prison being interrogated by the head of Crimes of Special Importance?

"Were you on the platform at the 'Kirpichnaya' train stop before sunrise on October 31, 1990, and, if so, what were you doing there?"

Kostoev slapped that card down on the table because it was one of the few in his hand which had any value. Three witnesses had seen a tall, slope-shouldered man in glasses, with a bandaged finger, suddenly emerge from the woods and take his place with them on the platform. It was four A.M. Those three early-shift workers took that train every day and there was never anyone else waiting. They found the man frightening, the way he limped and hobbled as if injured.

Kostoev knew that on the previous evening Chikatilo had killed his next-to-last victim, Victor Tishchenko, the strong, athletic boy who he suspected had bitten off the end of Chikatilo's finger and might also have injured his leg in the struggle.

What had Chikatilo been doing for all those hours between the evening killing and his appearance at that remote stop at four in the morning?

"No," said Chikatilo, "I was not at the 'Kirpichnaya' stop on October 31, 1990."

It was the perfect answer, just what Kostoev wanted. If he had said, yes, sure, I was there, so what, that would have shown him a truly masterful player. And that strategy, pursued to the end, would, as Kostoev was all too aware, prove invincible.

But Chikatilo had said no. And that told Kostoev everything he needed to know about the strength and cunning behind Chikatilo's denials.

"How often do you go to the town beach in Novocherkassk?" asked Kostoev matter-of-factly.

"I have never been to the beach in Novocherkassk. I don't even know where the beach is."

Kostoev gazed at him sadly, as if to say, Have our relations deteriorated so much that you'd think I'd believe you don't know where the beach in Novocherkassk is, when we both know exactly what you did to a boy in the reeds there?

Then, after a long pause, Kostoev asked with a tinge of anger in his voice: "Can you tell me where you were during the holidays of March 6, 7, and 8 in 1990?"

"On the holidays of March 6, 7, and 8, 1990, I was home in Novocherkassk and was not in Rostov on the Don."

Now Chikatilo was not only telling where he had been, but where he hadn't.

And where Chikatilo had been was the Botanical Gardens, with a boy he'd spotted bumming spare change and cigarettes in the Rostov train station, and whose heart he had torn out with his hands after slitting the boy open.

"Where and when did you acquire the jackknife confiscated from you when you were arrested? And why is it so sharp?"

"It was around 1987. I was making business trips to Sverdlov province in Siberia, to a nonferrous metal-processing plant in Kameno-Uralsk. The plant had a dormitory and that's where I found that Vixen brand knife. Since then I've carried that knife and use it for daily needs. I don't remember when and where I sharpened it the last time."

Kostoev was not interested in how Chikatilo had acquired the knife. Rather, he wanted to remind Chikatilo of a few murder sites and then bring the murder weapon back to mind. Chikatilo could answer the questions any way he wished, but it was Kostoev who would control the associations that came to Chikatilo's mind. It was Kostoev who could conduct the deep conversation while, far above, the questions and easy lies floated by.

And now it was time to show Chikatilo that he possessed information on his murders that reached back in time and to places other than Rostov.

"Were you in Moscow during the festival there in July 1985?"

"Yes, I was in Moscow during the festival in July 1985. I was there on business alone. I went to the Moskabel plant which is located in central Moscow. I was there on business for about two weeks. I lived in the Moskabel Plant's dormitory. I was at one mass demonstration at Dynamo Stadium. I traveled to Moscow and back home by train."

"Did you happen to be at Domodedovo Airport at any time?" asked Kostoev, for it was there in Moscow that Chikatilo had killed.

"I don't remember ever being at Domodedovo Airport."

Chikatilo was willing to admit that he was in Moscow at the time of the murder, but not that he might have been at the Moscow airport where the murder had occurred. As soon as a specific site was mentioned, he fled back into denial.

The odor was back, fainter but still hideously unique. This time Kostoev thought it could be compared to fried garlic, but that wasn't it either.

Kostoev wrote up a summation of the interrogation which Chikatilo found accurate and so indicated by signing his name at the bottom of the page beside Kostoev's. The lawyer left, but

Kostoev kept Chikatilo on for some conversation, nothing official, just between them.

"Weren't you wearing glasses last week, Andrei Romanovich?" asked Kostoev.

"No. Maybe one day. I don't wear glasses much anymore," answered Chikatilo, who, Kostoev saw to his satisfaction, had become suddenly aware that he had been observed through the peephole in his cell door.

"You know, Andrei Romanovich," began Kostoev in a somewhat distant tone, "I thought we had started working well together, but apparently I was mistaken."

Kostoev paused, not expecting Chikatilo to answer. He knew Chikatilo would not be foolish enough to engage him directly, as if the struggle between them ever ceased for a second.

Kostoev had deliberately invoked memories of murder in Chikatilo. The gravity of his crimes must weigh constantly on him and remind him of the reality of execution.

"Now it's going to be hard for me to believe you even when you're telling the truth. I don't need you to confess, Andrei Romanovich. You're the one who needs to confess and I've told you why," said Kostoev in the thinning tones of disappointment.

Allowing that last vision—hospitals, clean sheets, life itself—to linger for a moment in Chikatilo's mind, Kostoev brought the session to an abrupt close, saying: "The choice is yours, Andrei Romanovich."

CHAPTER 19

The T-shaped desk in KGB interrogation room 211 was so well polished that it reflected both Kostoev and Chikatilo, a doubled image like that on a figure card.

The odor seemed to have vanished.

"I've thought the situation over," said Chikatilo, in a tone that announced something new coming, "and I've decided to testify about my criminal activities. Please ask me specific questions."

"Tell me about your last murder, Svetlana Korostik," said Kostoev, remembering standing in the freezing rain yelling at the police who insisted that their men had been at their posts and had even picked up one suspect, a man who had been checked out before.

"I don't know Svetlana Korostik and I did not murder her," replied Chikatilo.

"Then what is it you mean by your 'criminal activities'?"

"In 1977, while working as a teacher of Russian language and literature in a boarding school in Novoshakhtinsk, I once kept some pupils after school. One of them was a girl named Tultseva, a sixth-grader I think. When she was alone in the classroom I went over to her with the intention of satisfying my sexual needs. I touched her breasts and may have even slapped her bottom. Then she started screaming. I locked her in the classroom, but she jumped out the window. The principal of the boarding school found about this incident and I was forced to leave my job.

"While I was still working at the boarding school, I took the students out on field trips fairly often, sometimes we went swimming at Kosikinsky Dam. There's a forest strip near that dam. One time I somehow took one of the girl students, Luba Koshkina, deep into the woods. When we were far away from everyone, I did in fact slip my hands into her clothing in the hope of some sort of sexual pleasure. She began resisting and screaming, and so nothing came of it.

"I want to point out that when I am in intimate circumstances with children, I am overcome by an unrestrainable passion, and practically cannot control my own behavior. Afterwards, I feel ill at ease about what I've done and I regret that I did it. I think this is connected with my mental problems."

Kostoev understood this double message. Chikatilo was covering what he said earlier about his "criminal activities," by now defining that to mean the child molestations in which he engaged in the seventies. He knew the investigation was aware of them. He had tidily removed the one inconsistency in his earlier testimony.

But, on the deeper level, Chikatilo was really continuing his confession of soul, if not deed. He was acknowledging the power of his sexual attraction to children.

Kostoev sensed that Chikatilo's instinct for self-preservation was powerful, but confused as to where self-preservation lay. In denial backed by partial admissions? Or in grasping insanity as his best defense and only hope?

After today there were only three days left. The pressure and tension would be at their zenith as the chance for Chikatilo to choose came for the very last time.

Kostoev judged it time to remind Chikatilo of another murder site.

"Have you ever been at a train stop called 'Izlovaisk'?"

asked Kostoev, playing that card with irked distraction as if the game were losing its savor for him.

"No, I have never been at that train stop."

Now Kostoev's bitter smile told Chikatilo that he was glad Chikatilo had not cooperated. Why should the man who had killed that nine-year-old boy in the forest strip by Izlovaisk station be allowed to live?

"When and how did you acquire your private car?" asked Kostoev, closing the subject of murder. And, as Chikatilo went on at length about when and how he had acquired his Mosk-vich 2140, Kostoev realized that in fact they'd talked enough. It was time for some theatrics.

CHAPTER 20

C hikatilo was startled, just as Kostoev had intended. It wasn't his lawyer he found in the room, but a photographer who was still fussing with his equipment as Chikatilo entered.

"Today," said Kostoev in a businesslike tone, "we are going to take some pictures of you, Andrei Romanovich."

With a movement of his head Kostoev indicated two sealed bags in one corner of the room.

"Those bags contain your clothes which we confiscated when we searched your apartment. I'll tell you which ones to wear and how to stand."

The message was clear, Kostoev was assuming direct physical command over Chikatilo. If he told Chikatilo to remove his clothes, Chikatilo would have to remove them. Another message was being transmitted to Chikatilo, that photographs were taken for one reason only—to show witnesses for purposes of identification. That, in turn, meant that Kostoev had lost all hope in Chikatilo cooperating, and was therefore now returning to the evidentiary side of the case.

The photographer was ready.

"Alright then, please stand up, Andrei Romanovich, and remove your overalls. I'll prepare the first set of clothes."

Kostoev sat and watched Chikatilo take off his black labor-camp overalls. Through his obedience Chikatilo had been made to feel the power of the Soviet state and of Kostoev's personality, and the full weight of the case against him.

Chikatilo was naked now except for his shorts and prison slippers. Once again Kostoev's eyes went to Chikatilo's elongated nipples, so much like Slivko's that he had to wonder whether it was only coincidence that the two child-dismemberers shared such a rare trait.

"These first, Andrei Romanovich," said Kostoev, handing him the first set of clothes.

Chikatilo stepped resentfully into the brown pants.

Good, thought Kostoev, let him be unhappy. I'll be unhappy with him, he'll be unhappy with me.

Chikatilo pulled on a gray shirt and began buttoning it.

"And the cap," Kostoev ordered.

Chikatilo placed the cap carelessly on his head.

"Face the camera," said Kostoev, watching to make sure Chikatilo complied before nodding to the photographer.

"Now put on this hat," said Kostoev, wanting to move quickly. The flash continually going off in Chikatilo's face would shock his nerves.

"Now this one."

Another flash lit the bare room.

"Now with these pants and this shirt."

Chikatilo was more aware of the photographer as he undressed a second time. Kostoev was making him stand naked in front of a stranger.

Kostoev smiled when he saw Chikatilo grimace to distort his features and make his face harder to identify. But nobody was ever going to see those pictures. The witnesses had already identified him from the photographs taken on the day of his arrest.

Suddenly Chikatilo glared directly into the lens, aiming his vengeful hatred at the photographer, only the latest to do him injustice.

Andrei Chikatilo
in 1958, at age 22.

Inspector Issa Kostoev.

Chikatilo with his wife, Feodosia ("Fenya"), and son, Yuri, in 1970.

Inspector Kostoev with his five children at home in Moscow.

Chikatilo with his daughter, Ludmila, his son-in-law, and granddaughter.

Inspector Yandiev.

Vladimir Storozhenko, serial killer
caught by Kostoev in 1981.

Chikatilo at 54.

Town of Shakhty.

Steps leading up to and interior of the "secret house," where
Chikatilo committed his first murder in 1978.

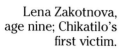

Lena Zakotnova, age nine; Chikatilo's first victim.

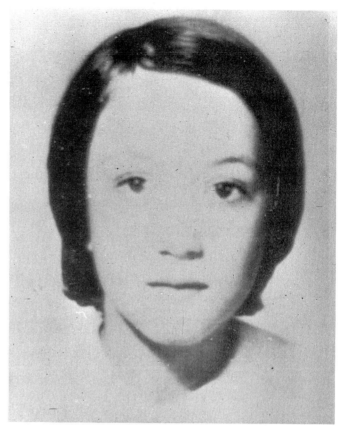

Murder weapon. One of 23 knives used by Chikatilo.

Grushevka River,
where the first victim,
Lena Zakotnova,
was thrown.

Bridge over
Grushevka River,
beneath which
Lena Zakotnova's
body was found.

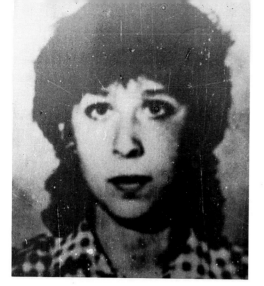

Ludmilla Alekseeva, seventeen
years old, one of Chikatilo's
fifteen victims in 1984.

Elena Varga,
nineteen-year-old
Hungarian student
killed by Chikatilo
on his way to visit
his dying father.

Aleksei Khobotov,
ten years old, buried by
Chikatilo in the Shakhty
Municipal Cemetery.

Victor Petrov, age 14,
whose skeletalized
remains were found in
the Rostov Botanical
Gardens.

ТИШЕНКО
ВИКТОР НИКОЛАЕВИЧ
15.04.74г.р. урожен. г.Шахты
ушел из дома 30.10.90г. в12ч.
Рост 165см.,волос светлый,
волнистый,глаза серые,нос
прямой,губы толстые,
при разговоре шепелявит.

Одет:
куртка из ткани "Болонья"
коричневая, рубашка серая
с длинным рукавом,брюки
школьные синие,кроссовки се-
рого цвета.

Особые приметы:
косоглазие правого глаза

Missing persons report on Victor Tishchenko,
next-to-last victim.

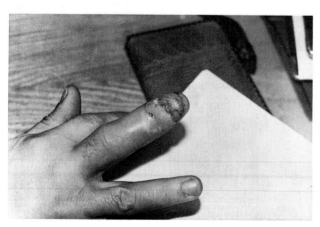

Chikatilo's finger, bitten
by Victor Tishchenko.

Platform and passenger
shelter at "Tree Farm"
station, where Chikatilo
was stopped by police
in November 1990.

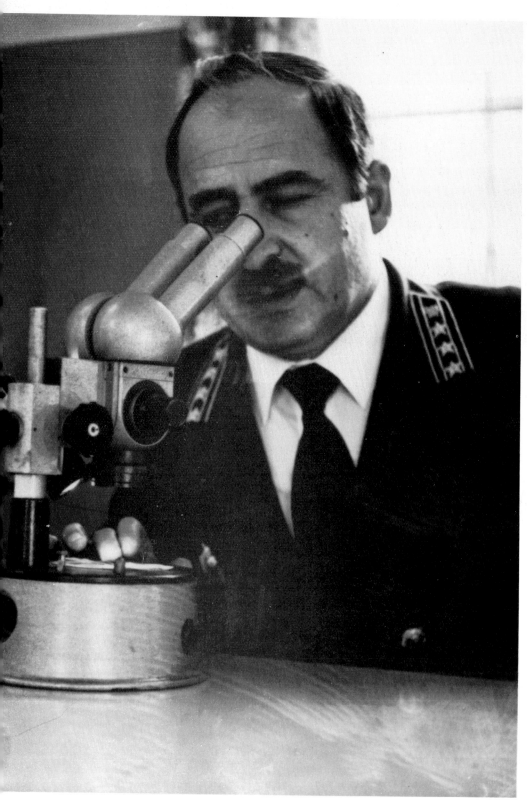

Inspector Kostoev in the crime lab.

Adjoining Rostov Police and KGB headquarters,
where Chikatilo was questioned and held.

Composite sketches
and personal items
confiscated from
Chikatilo after his arrest.

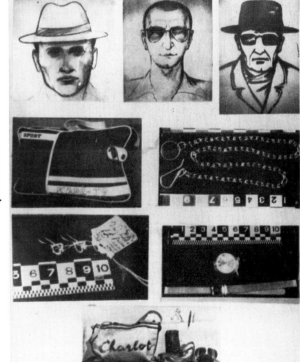

Mugshot of Chikatilo
on the day of his arrest,
November 20, 1990.

Kostoev questioning
Chikatilo in the office of
General Fetisov, Rostov Police.

Russian-style lineup; Chikatilo at far right.

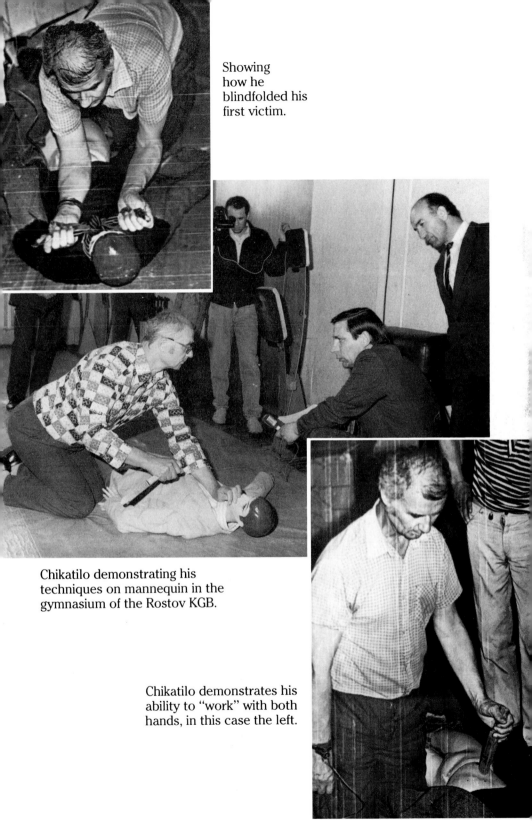

Showing
how he
blindfolded his
first victim.

Chikatilo demonstrating his
techniques on mannequin in the
gymnasium of the Rostov KGB.

Chikatilo demonstrates his
ability to "work" with both
hands, in this case the left.

Kostoev interrogating Chikatilo.
The eighth day in Room 211.

"This cap."

"This hat."

Even as he barked orders, Kostoev still managed to occupy the moral high ground of the injured party. He had shown Chikatilo his trust, had confided in him that he could not believe him sane, no sane man could ever have done what he'd done. He had offered Chikatilo the chance of help, treatment, a reasonable and humane offer that had been suicidally spurned.

Kostoev could see that Chikatilo was weakening. The result of choosing an inferior strategy. And of being humiliated by Kostoev. But Kostoev also knew that this was a man fighting for his life, and in a position stronger than he knew.

"Sit down," said Kostoev, "I want this one of you sitting."

The walls of the room were reverberating with flashes.

"Alright, we're done. You can put your overalls back on."

Chikatilo would have to undress one more time, feel the vulnerability of the naked. Kostoev watched, the photographer packed up his equipment.

"Thank you," said Kostoev to the photographer. "And, don't forget, I want them developed immediately.

"You won't need your lawyer today, Andrei Romanovich, because I have no intention of questioning you," said Kostoev, fully aware of what such a statement would mean to a suspect on the eighth day of questioning, when no confession has been obtained. Signaling Kostoev's intention to return to the realm of evidence, it was, as much as anything, a farewell.

"Still, there is one thing I would like to say, Andrei Romanovich. I don't understand why you choose not to cooperate. From speaking with you I know that you are an intelligent man. And I do believe I explained everything quite clearly to you.

"As I've told you, you're not the first murderer I've ever sat with in a room like this. And you won't be the last. Because this is what I do with my life, Andrei Romanovich, I sit with people like you and try to help put them back in touch with life and people. But you had even more to gain than that. You had a choice between treatment and execution. And if you were cured, do you think they'd keep you in the hospital or put you in prison? No. You'd be a free man, alive and free. Are you really so twisted, Andrei Romanovich, that you would prefer death to that?"

Kostoev spoke evenly but there was doom in his voice, the doom of iron doors slamming in brick walls, blast of a pistol behind the ear.

Chikatilo disappeared into his silence. But this time it was not only a retreat from the unbearable pressures of the bare interrogation room. Chikatilo was going to make his decision now. If he waited until tomorrow, the ninth day, it might be too late.

Chikatilo emerged from his silence, though still without saying a word.

In the formal tone of voice used to conclude proceedings, Kostoev asked: "Do you have any complaints or requests, Andrei Romanovich?"

Chikatilo hesitated for a moment, then burst into the sobs that precede confession, his soul streaming toward the freedom only truth can give.

"I would like to write out my statement," said Chikatilo when he could speak, his tone that of a man so emotionally exhausted that even speech was an effort.

"Is it going to be the same thing again, without any details?" asked Kostoev.

"No," said Chikatilo, "I understand everything now."

Kostoev sat and watched Chikatilo write, the top of his scalp visible through his thinning hair. He did not want to interfere with the writing but still wanted his presence constantly felt to remind Chikatilo not to escape into the autobiographical.

Chikatilo covered four sheets of paper. After signing his

name in the bottom right-hand corner, Chikatilo handed those four sheets to Kostoev.

"After my arrest, I have been questioned several times and asked to speak about my criminal activities. My inconsistent behavior should not be judged as any attempt to evade responsibility for what I have wrought. Some people may think that, after my arrest, I have not been cognizant of the danger and gravity of what I have done. I want to be believed when I say that is not so at all. My case is by nature exceptional.

"It is not the fear of taking responsibility that forced me to act that way but the intensity, the pressure on my nerves and psyche. I don't know why but everyone considered me an idiot. I always thought people underestimated me, but those who don't agree always treat me strangely, without logic or justice. I tortured myself writing complaints. I took all that tension inside me. And that made for nightmares and insomnia. The charges brought against me fill me with horror. I can not bear being conscious of all that and expressing it. I think my heart would burst. I've wanted to be cured for a long time, but I didn't seek help. . . . Everything irritated me, all those conversations about the weather, is it good, is it bad. I carried all that fury inside myself and found no way to vent it. If possible, I would like my psyche to be treated, if it is abnormal. Then I could help the investigation establish the truth and I could bear the punishment I deserve. I am ready to testify about the crimes I have committed but I do request that you not torment me with details and specifics. My mind could not bear it. After treatment I will attempt to reconstruct everything from memory."

Kostoev looked up at Chikatilo to gauge his sincerity. Chikatilo meant it. Chikatilo was broken.

CHAPTER 21

I promise not to torment you with details and specifics," said Kostoev the next day, quoting Chikatilo's own words back to him. Indeed, Kostoev had no intention of delving into all the minutiae and particulars of the case, that he would leave to Yandiev. What he wanted was a signed confession to specific murders and new, substantiatable evidence provided by Chikatilo himself, a clincher known in Kostoev's trade as the "big nail."

Kostoev was not going to interrogate him that day but he wanted time with Chikatilo, to maintain contact and to check for the slightest signs of backsliding, of which there were none. Kostoev had also arranged a very pleasant surprise for Chikatilo, a reward, a reassurance, a taste of hope.

Chikatilo had been unable to resist hope—serious doctors in white coats listening to his every word, food, newspapers, life.

When he had visited Slivko on death row, Kostoev had presented himself as a "physician from Moscow," but obviously he himself could not play that role this time. Recalling Bukhanovsky, the psychiatric specialist in transsexualism who had been checked out himself before beginning to consult with the Rostov police, Kostoev called police headquarters and arranged for Bukhanovsky to appear that day at the KGB prison.

Kostoev met Bukhanovsky in another part of the prison where the psychiatrist would wait until summoned to Room 211. Bukhanovsky was a tall and imposing man, sallow and jowly, with black hair and sideburns, and compassionate eyes.

"The conversation must be kept general. Nothing you say must contradict Chikatilo's belief that criminals like him can be found legally insane, and sent for treatment instead of execution," said Kostoev. Receiving agreement, he returned to Room 211 to await the prisoner.

"Andrei Romanovich," said Kostoev in the buoyant tone of those about to dispense largesse, "I have invited a specialist here today to see you. You may ask any questions you might have about your condition. His name is Alexander Olympievich Bukhanovsky, deputy head of the psychiatric faculty at the University of Rostov."

"Yes, I would like to meet with him," replied Chikatilo. "I really do think my mind has been destroyed. Some of the things I did while committing my crimes, later on I couldn't understand them myself."

Bukhanovsky was summoned.

Kostoev noted the time, 2:35, in the record of the interrogation, as stipulated by regulations.

After introductions and a few minutes' talk, Chikatilo said: "I would like the chance of speaking with Dr. Bukhanovsky alone."

"Of course," said Kostoev.

Kostoev left the room and used the time to think how to convince Chikatilo to divulge evidence that would stand up in court even if he recanted his entire confession at some later point. An about-face like that was never out of the question, especially with someone like Chikatilo. Kostoev was certain that Chikatilo would begin to confess in detail tomorrow, the tenth day, but it would take at least a week to go over all thirty-six murders. Only then would Kostoev be able to take him to one murder site or another in search of the "big nail."

After about an hour and a half, Kostoev decided it was time to go back. Chikatilo would have gotten a good taste of the future he had chosen for himself, though the point was only to whet his appetite.

After allowing the conversation to wind down, Kostoev had Chikatilo and Bukhanovsky sign the record where it indicated that their conversation had lasted from 2:35 to 4:15.

After Bukhanovsky left, Kostoev spent a few minutes alone with Chikatilo, asking questions—was it interesting, was it useful?—the answers to which did not interest him in the least. All he wanted was a clear read on Chikatilo's mood and state of mind. The attention of a psychiatrist and the release of imminent confession had elevated and enlivened Chikatilo with hope and peace. Only fitting, thought Kostoev, that it be hope and peace that doom him.

CHAPTER 22

I t was Chikatilo's turn to surprise Kostoev, and surprise him twice, on the tenth day, November 30, 1990.

"These two aren't mine," said Chikatilo, having carefully read the detailed list of charges against him, "but I admit to the rest."

"Which two?" asked Kostoev, leaning forward to the list.

Chikatilo had no reason to lie about those two murders and seemed sincere in his resolute denial. Kostoev detected a certain smugness in Chikatilo now. As if he had won out in the end, outsmarted Kostoev, duped him into believing he was a person needing and worthy of help. Kostoev could not let on that this was exactly what he had wanted. The best ironies were for the investigator alone.

"Alright," said Kostoev, "I accept that. Those two aren't yours, but the rest are, is that correct?"

"Yes," answered Chikatilo.

"Then sign here."

Chikatilo signed.

"And now let's begin from the beginning," said Kostoev, who, having 1982 in mind as the year of the first murder, was about to receive his second surprise of the day.

"I had bought a little house on Border Lane in Shakhty. I was planning to fix the place up and put in a garden. . . . I don't remember the exact date but it was an evening at the end of December 1978. I got off at the Grushevka Bridge streetcar stop, the one nearest the house on Border Lane. It was late in the day and getting dark. I started heading toward my house. To my surprise I noticed a girl of about eleven or twelve with a school case who was walking in the same direction I was. For a little while we walked side by side down the dark, unlit street by the river. I struck up a conversation with the girl. I remember she said she was going to see a friend.

"When we came near the tall reeds that grow by the river and were a distance from the nearest houses, an irresistible urge to have sexual relations with that girl came over me. I don't know what happened to me, but I literally began shaking. I stopped the girl and threw her down into the reeds. She tried to struggle free but I was literally in a state of animal frenzy, I couldn't stop myself, I pulled off her pants and began thrusting my hands into her sexual organs. At the same time, to keep her quiet, I began squeezing her throat. I began ripping at her sexual organs. I had an orgasm while lying on top of her and tearing her sexual organs. I did not have intercourse as such with her. The sperm either went between her legs or on her stomach.

"When I realized the girl was dead, I dressed her and threw her body in the river. Then I threw her school case in too. I washed my hands and put my clothes in order. Then I returned to the streetcar stop, and went home . . .

"This was my first crime and I sincerely regretted it . . . What happened that night made a very strong impression on me. I can even say that I don't remember the moment when I ejaculated. All I remember clearly is that tearing at her sexual organs caused me a tremendous sensation. I can't describe it any more precisely, but it was real. I was in some kind of frenzy, ruled by some sort of bestial passion. It was only when I had regained some calm that I realized she was dead. A few days later I was called in for questioning. The police asked me where

I was on the night of the murder. I said I had been home and my wife verified this. I was aware that someone else was arrested for this crime.

"After that first murder I think my psyche underwent certain definite changes. I was haunted by the image of my hands tearing the girl's organs apart, I couldn't get it out of my mind."

Kostoev was stunned, elated, worried. Chikatilo was telling more than they had known, but what happened to that person who had been arrested for Chikatilo's first murder?

Kostoev's mind instantly fixated on that question and he was relieved when, after describing a second murder, Chikatilo declared himself tired and requested a recess until the next day.

An investigation into the first murder had to be launched at once.

Over the next five days, Chikatilo gave short descriptions of all his murders, indicating only the most essential features—time, place, and manner of contact, actual site of the crime, type of wounds inflicted. But he also spoke of the urges even he could not understand.

"When murdering women, I'd have the desire to get inside their abdomen, to cut out their sexual organs and throw them away. I cannot explain why that desire came to me. I did in fact slice open the stomachs of my victims and cut out the uterus and other organs attached to it."

He was not ready yet to discuss precisely what he had done with those body parts.

Chikatilo stressed that he was overwhelmed by forces beyond his control, and that sometimes, when leaving the scene of a crime, he was so disconnected from reality that he would walk in front of oncoming cars. Kostoev didn't believe it for a minute. This was a man who cleaned the crime site so thoroughly that not a scrap of evidence had ever been found. This was a man who, after killing a woman, had struck up a friendly conversation with the mushroom gatherers who'd taken refuge from the rain at the shelter at Tree Farm station. This was a man who had secret apartments and carried a change of clothes. But all that could be refuted later. There was a much more pressing issue now, the question of hard evidence; on the evening of December 6, Kostoev knew how to get the "big nail."

Nothing could be more true of Ingush culture than respect for the dead, some of Kostoev's countrymen had even brought their relatives' bones back from exile in Kazakhstan to bury them in home soil. And so Kostoev was entirely sincere that evening when he said: "You know, Andrei Romanovich, I'm a religious man. And in my religion there is nothing more terrible than a body that has not been properly buried. And so if there are any bodies we don't know about, we should take care of them right away, it just isn't human for them not to be properly buried."

"In the Shakhty Municipal Cemetery," said Chikatilo, "I dug a grave for myself at a time when I was considering suicide. But, in the end, it was one of my victims I buried there."

"Can you show me where?" asked Kostoev.

"Yes, but I'd be afraid people would see me."

"You don't have to be afraid. We'll do it in the evening and you'll be protected by police bodyguards."

Chikatilo was hesitant. For seventeen days, he had been alone in that room with Kostoev, and now the thought of going out into the world had a fearful, overwhelming quality about it.

"Don't worry," said Kostoev, "you'll be as safe as you are here."

On the evening of December 7, Kostoev and Chikatilo drove to Shakhty accompanied by several policemen, one of whom had a video camera. It was dark as they approached the city, the huge mountains of slag in the outlying fields barely visible against the December sky.

Walking between gravestones which displayed a photographic likeness of the deceased and past plots fenced in like little parks, Chikatilo brought them directly to the site.

Then the only sound was that of shovels and the faint whir-ring of the video camera. Finally, a child's sneaker emerged through the earth. The camera zoomed in on it. Chikatilo was a dead man.

PART V

I t may or may not be true that the image of the murderer is imprinted on the victim's eyes, but it was certainly true that the image of Chikatilo's victims had been imprinted on his own memory. Even after twelve years he had no difficulty in selecting the photograph of his first victim, Lena Zakotnova, from a group of photographs of other dark-haired nine-year-old girls. He did the same with all his victims, many of whose names he was learning only now.

Chikatilo also displayed an excellent memory for place, never more than a few yards off when he was taken to a site, outings known in the trade as "*vyvodki*," a word that also means stain removal and the exercising of animals. He did once lie about location but only for the best of reasons. When Kostoev informed him that his immediate family and closest relatives had been safely removed from Rostov Province and supplied with new identities and homes, Chikatilo admitted that he had not killed his first victim in the reeds by the river but in his own house at 26 Border Lane. He had relatives in Shakhty and was concerned for their safety. Now that this was no longer an issue, Chikatilo wanted to clean up the point, a pedantic tidiness one of the characteristics that had survived all the transformations of his psyche. He had even begun working out a system to classify his victims. Each category had its own initial,

EM, easy morals, D, drifter, A, adolescent, R, retarded. He applied the suitable letter or combination of letters to each of his victims. A few bore all the characteristics, EMDARs.

On December 11, 1990, three weeks after his arrest, Chikatilo surprised Kostoev yet again.

"One thing I want to impress upon you, Andrei Romanovich," said Kostoev. "When the investigation is completed, you will be sent to the Serbsky Psychiatric Institute in Moscow for prolonged study. You'll be dealing with highly qualified and experienced people. If during that process you should confess to any other crimes, that would reflect very badly on you. So, if there are any other murders you may have committed, now, Andrei Romanovich, is the time to remember them."

As if he had only been waiting to be asked, Chikatilo summoned the memory of another eleven. The number shocked and chilled Kostoev. And it also meant more teams, more investigations, more trips out to the field. And the following day Chikatilo suddenly recalled his second murder, that of the wild girl in the claret-red jacket, Larisa Tkachenko, whom he had taken to the left bank of the Don in the hope of normal passion.

At first he mixed up the dates, placing the murder much later in time. But then he remembered it had been in 1981 when he was just starting out, before it had all become, as he put it, "almost routine."

The murders themselves did not appear to interest Chikatilo greatly, his favorite subject was himself. He had begun work on a long autobiographical essay Kostoev jocularly termed Chikatilo's "Talmud." Chikatilo also had practical reasons for writing. He was building his own case for insanity. Still, Kostoev knew, there was more to it than that—Chikatilo was also lost in the rapture that comes upon a person when every detail of his life and person becomes of monumental interest to another.

In the course of the interrogation Chikatilo cleared up some of the smaller mysteries like that of the tree trunk that had been stabbed. Chikatilo said that sometimes even amputation and orgasm afforded him no ultimate relief and he had to discharge the last of his fury against a tree.

He explained the reasoning behind some of the wounds he inflicted: "The lips are associated with the sexual organs. And I get a kind of sexual pleasure from injuring lips." And he also admitted: "I vented my full fury for revenge on the genitals of my victims."

But Kostoev was sure that Chikatilo was not being fully candid in response to certain questions. Like Slivko, Chikatilo had certain odd points of pride. Slivko had insisted there was nothing fascistic about his fetishism. Chikatilo was squeamish about describing the full extent of his cannibalism.

Kostoev pressed him on the point. "Andrei Romanovich, your wife has testified that you often took a pot or pan with you even though you can't cook. Traces of campfires were found near some of your victims."

"I liked to nibble on a uterus, they're so pink and springy," admitted Chikatilo. "But after nibbling them, I'd throw them away."

"None were ever found."

Chikatilo shrugged.

He would not yield the secrets of his craft of allurement.

"Maybe there's something magnetic about me, I don't know. All I ever said was, 'I know a shortcut, come to my dacha.'"

Taken to the KGB gymnasium to be interviewed and video-taped while demonstrating his techniques for subduing and killing his victims, Chikatilo was very lackadaisical, almost ab-sentminded. Having previously described his knife thrusts as wild and out of his control, he now poked the mannequin listlessly with a wooden knife. Kostoev knew that both Chikatilo's description and demonstration were deceptive. Many of the wounds had been inflicted at a tormentingly slow pace, while others had been delivered in a fury as he lay on the body of a woman or child and, as he put it, did a "pitiable imitation of the sex act."

He did keep on remembering murders, reaching a final total of fifty-five. He still spoke of them as if relating how he'd gone to the store and bought bread. Kostoev observed that Chikatilo made a point of using passive and impersonal forms in his speech. It was not something he'd done, something had happened to him. His throat would go dry, forces would overwhelm him. Then he, a man whom his son had described as someone "who went pale at the sight of a drop of his own blood," would become a maniac for whom blood was the most exciting of sights.

The compulsion could come over him any time. He had murdered on the way to visit his dying father and on his way to his son's trial for petty theft.

Kostoev saw it somewhat differently. Chikatilo was constantly hunting, but would make his move only when he was sure it was safe, even if that meant waiting years.

By mid-December Chikatilo had supplied ample hard evidence, and a press conference was called to make a formal public announcement of the capture and confession. There was some jockeying for credit at the press conference, though the head of the Rostov Police had paid full homage to Kostoev as "deserving the principal credit for solving the case." Still, it struck Kostoev that the Rostov Police were claiming more credit than appropriate for an organization which had arrested Chikatilo in 1984 and released him, preferring to think they had already apprehended the killers, a group of mentally retarded youths. They had not even thought to take a semen sample from such a promising suspect. And the files concerning that arrest had never been made available to Kostoev until he had demanded them in November 1990. Kostoev was not certain whether this had been a matter of gross negligence, or whether the Rostov Police had deliberately covered up their fatal blunders. In either case, he fully intended to launch an investigation of the matter after Chikatilo had been sentenced.

Throughout December Kostoev continued to be the only person interrogating Chikatilo.

"How did you choose your victims, Andrei Romanovich?"

"I didn't chose them any special way, just whatever was at hand," said Chikatilo.

"But you never chose men, old women, old men. You chose children and drifters almost all the time."

"Well, yes, if you put it like that then that's true," said Chikatilo, who had a tendency to close discussions by agreeing. But he did not always accede. He was adamant that he had "never taken any of his victims' property for personal gain," and was insulted by any accusation of theft. Even though semen had been found in the mouth of one victim, Chikatilo denied ever forcing any of his victims to perform oral sex. "I would have been afraid to, they were in such agony, anything could happen." In that case, Kostoev grudgingly had to admit that the logic of life was on Chikatilo's side.

On December 27, 1990, Kostoev was handed a thick file on Alexander Kravchenko, the man who had been indicted for Chikatilo's first murder, but he was not able to look at that file until that evening when he was done questioning Chikatilo for the day.

Kostoev put on the glasses he needed now and began reading. Kravchenko had been sentenced to death for the rape and murder of the nine-year-old Shakhty schoolgirl, Lena Zakotnova, but that sentence had been reduced to fifteen years by the Russian Federation's Supreme Court. This clemency infuriated the girl's grandmother, Vera Zakotnova, who began bombarding government agencies with letters of outrage. She wrote to the editor of *Pravda,* the Committee of Soviet Women, and addressed a particularly passionate plea to the 26th Party Congress, saying:

"Kravchenko, the murderer of my granddaughter, tormented the girl and threw her body in the Grushevka River. And this scum, this useless man, this monster has been rewarded for his merits with the gift of life. Help me remove this monster, this scum from the face of the earth, a man who's already murdered two girls."

Her plea was heard. The sentence was overturned and the original death sentence reinstated by a Soviet judicial collegium, a decision then approved by both the Supreme Court of Russia and that of Rostov Province. Kostoev read quick snatches of Kravchenko's plea for mercy written in a neat and respectful hand. The last document was a small piece of paper, much signed, much stamped. Under the heading *Secret* it read: "The sentence passed by the judicial collegium in regard to the verdict rendered by the Rostov Province Court on March 23, 1982, condemning the accused, Alexander Kravchenko, born 1953, to capital punishment . . . was carried out on 5 July 1983."

"The bastards!" shouted Kostoev, alone in his office. He had been on death row with genuine murderers and felt the weight of their dread, but at least they had the solace of guilt.

Kostoev jumped up from his desk and went to the next office where another inspector was also working late.

"Give me a cigarette," said Kostoev.

"You don't smoke, you gave it up."

"Give me a cigarette," insisted Kostoev.

And he was back in five minutes for another one.

C H A P T E R   2 4

I n January 1991, Kostoev let Yandiev take over the questioning of Chikatilo while he researched the tragic fiasco of Alexander Kravchenko's execution.

The courts which had sentenced him to death would not easily be persuaded to admit their error. Kostoev knew he would have to make a case that was irrefutably strong and clear. And even that might not be enough.

But he had Chikatilo's detailed description of the murder of Zakotnova, his memory still vivid about the wounds he'd inflicted. Chikatilo had also been videotaped walking the short distance from his secret house on Border Lane to the vacant lot beside the house where Alexander Kravchenko had lived. As he walked, Chikatilo carried the mannequin of a little girl to the small rise that overlooked a tangle of cattails, then demonstrated how he had hurled the body into the river and where he tossed her school case.

Kravchenko's wife and her friend who had spent the evening with them were now ready to testify that they had changed their testimony under duress. And it could also be demonstrated that an underworld figure, Miroshnichenko, had been specially placed in Kravchenko's cell with the object of beating a confession out of him, since this could no longer be done directly by the police themselves as it had been in the old days.

Though Kostoev gave considerable attention to bringing Kravchenko's case to the courts, so that the sentence could be overturned and be made part of his indictment against Chikatilo, he also kept a close watch on the various interrogations that were being conducted simultaneously, chief among them Yandiev's of Chikatilo himself.

Before assuming control of Chikatilo, Yandiev had interrogated Chikatilo's wife, Fenya, and had spent so much time with her that Kostoev even began making suggestive jokes on the subject.

But the real reason was that Fenya Chikatilo was so terrified that she could barely speak. Terrified of the future that lay before her and her children. Terrified by what her husband had done. And even more terrified that anyone should think she had any part in it.

Yandiev complained that all she gave him was "a teaspoonful at a time." When Fenya had become convinced that her husband was indeed the killer, she had wanted to renounce him. "I don't want to see him again, I don't know who the man is, I don't even want to talk about him!"

But as Kostoev kept reminding Yandiev, "It's important that she doesn't renounce him, Chikatilo has to know he still has a family." If Chikatilo were plunged into gloom at the thought of being renounced by his family, he would turn from a fairly willing participant to one so deeply distracted as to be of little further use to the investigation.

Chikatilo was allowed to write to his wife every so often, a privilege that could be retracted. "The brightest thing in my life is you, my pure, beloved, sacred wife. Why didn't I obey you, dear, when you told me—work near home, don't take jobs that make you travel. Why didn't you place me under house arrest—didn't I always submit to you. Now I'd be home on my knees before you, praying to you, light of my life.

"How could have I sunk to such brutality, to such a primordial state, when everything around me was so pure and exalted. I've cried away my tears during these nights. Why did God send me to this earth, me, a person so affectionate, tender, and thoughtful, but totally defenseless against my own weaknesses . . ."

Yandiev convinced Fenya to write short notes back to her husband in prison. Sometimes she was so paralyzed by the thought of addressing that man, even the simplest of words would not come to her mind, and Yandiev would have to dictate the text: she was fine, their daughter was fine, and so was their son.

"That's all she wrote?" asked Chikatilo, both gladdened and downcast by the first note.

"That's all she's allowed to," said Yandiev, pleased to see Chikatilo compliantly accepting the sway of regulations.

At another point Yandiev arranged for money that Chikatilo had in a savings account to be transferred to Fenya, who had lost not only a husband and an entire life, but an income as well. Chikatilo had to compose a document transferring the money to her and she had to take that document to the bank. That too kept the Chikatilo family in touch, and intact.

When Yandiev felt the interrogation of Chikatilo (which had been going on almost two months now) begin to flag, he decided to put his long acquaintanceship with Fenya Chikatilo to good use.

"I'd like you to meet with your husband," said Yandiev.

Fenya refused categorically. "I won't go there to that KGB prison, people will see me going in there, and then everyone will say that I knew everything all the time. I won't go!"

But Yandiev knew how to play on her greatest fear, complicity. Without saying so directly, he let Fenya know that it was still what the investigators thought of her that was the most important thing, even though both he and Kostoev con-

sidered her totally innocent, naive almost to the point of sim-
plemindedness. In the end, Fenya relented.

A tall, brown-haired country woman, Fenya dressed up for
the meeting. As they waited for Chikatilo to be brought to the
visitors' room, Yandiev told Fenya to speak only about the
family and to say that everyone was alright. Yandiev kept her
engaged in conversation to help her control the welter of feelings that he could not even begin to imagine.

Chikatilo was brought in. Head bowed, he walked over to
his wife, put his arms around her, and kissed her on the neck
with a smacking salivary sound that reminded Yandiev of a
kitten clumsily seeking its mother's nipple.

Then they stood apart, Fenya regarding him with a searching gaze that he would not meet.

"How could you have, Andrei?"

"Fenya, Fenechka, it's how it turned out. You were always
telling me I should see a doctor, but I didn't obey you, I didn't
obey you."

Chikatilo cringed as if expecting a blow from her.

"It's true," Yandiev interjected to ease the tension of the
moment and again to dangle the promise of medical treatment
to Chikatilo. "He does need treatment, and it won't be too very
long before he's in the Serbsky Institute."

"And how's Yurka?" asked Chikatilo, using the family name
for their son, Yuri. He asked the question softly in a guilty tone
of voice, as if to acknowledge that any question he asked was
by definition monstrous.

"Yurka's fine," said Fenya, "but he's been disobedient."

Yandiev thought the detail of the son's disobedience,
though slightly negative in itself, was still basically good, just
the sort of thing families normally do talk about. Yandiev also
knew that the truth behind Fenya's remark was that their son
was now being seized by outbursts of rage against his father
and mother. "If you hadn't married that man, he wouldn't be
my father!"

The son had a girlfriend he could never see again, and nothing to look forward to but a life of concealments. The daughter, Ludmila, could never accept in her heart that the man who took her daughter, his granddaughter, out for walks was the same man who had taken other children out for other walks.

The meeting was kept short. Fenya's nerves could not be trusted. And, at this stage, Chikatilo deserved just enough of a taste of his wife's company to feed his dream of being cured and rejoining Fenya at the end of his days.

Chikatilo and Fenya parted as they had greeted each other, with an awkward embrace, his eyes never once having met hers.

"Hello," said Kostoev, picking up the phone in his office in Rostov.

The call was from the guard escorting Chikatilo to a murder site. "We can't find the body. We even flew over in a helicopter."

"Is the prisoner there?" asked Kostoev.

"Yes."

"Put him on."

"I looked and I looked," said Chikatilo plaintively, "but it's been so many years, and they've built something here."

"Listen to me, you son of a bitch!" bellowed Kostoev. "After all I've done for you, you better not come back here without that fucking corpse!"

Then he immediately slammed down the phone so that Chikatilo would not hear him roaring with laughter; only in the black comedies of his profession could a person order a cannibal to find a corpse.

The first protest against Kravchenko's death sentence, written by Kostoev and presented by the Russian Attorney General, was rejected, and a second had to be written. It was a slow process, one measured in months, and by the time spring came to Rostov the second protest had still not been passed on. Chikatilo's interrogation began to wind down in July 1991. By then it had also been fully supplemented by testimony from those who knew him in his native Ukrainian village, those who remembered him from school, the people he'd served with in the army, his students, his colleagues, and other coworkers; one woman who had shared an office with him in 1984, during the peak of the killings, remembered a terrible odor coming from him then, one unlike anything she had ever smelled before.

Two hundred and twenty-five volumes of evidence and testimony had been assembled. Now it was time for Kostoev to write up the indictment. That meant distilling the essentials into a single volume that would, with lucid, iron logic, make the case for each of the fifty-three of the fifty-five murders that could be substantiated and the five charges of child molestation brought against Chikatilo. This final task could not be completed until he had the findings of the Serbsky Institute, to which Chikatilo would be transferred in August and where he would spend approximately three months.

But Kostoev could work both on the indictment and the protest of the verdict on Kravchenko at home in Moscow. To pack his things, he returned one last time to Room 339 in the Hotel Rostov where the rule had been, no cold water in the summer, and in winter no hot.

The willow was now high over his balcony, a green lament of foliage.

The Soviet Union plunged into crisis on August 19 of that year, 1991, when a small group of the highest government officials placed Soviet President Gorbachev under house arrest at his dacha in the south, while seizing power for themselves. The asphalt on the streets of Moscow was chewed up by tanks heading for the White House, headquarters of Boris Yeltsin,

President of Russia, and, unlike Gorbachev, elected to that post. It was a showdown between Russia and the Soviet Union.

On the second day of the coup, when the citizens of Moscow were coming out of their shock and beginning to gather in outrage and build barricades around the White House, Andrei Chikatilo was delivered to the Serbsky Institute, the car bearing him from the airport able to avoid the tanks and chaos which were concentrated at a few specific points.

Chikatilo was seen by a battery of psychiatrists, six of whom would sign the findings of the Serbsky Institute that would take more than three months to issue. While the initial tests were being performed on Chikatilo, determining that he did indeed suffer from organic impotence, the battle in the streets of Moscow reached its apogee. Yeltsin rallied the country from the top of a tank, just as Lenin had once done from the top of an armored car. The KGB did not attack as planned, and the regular troops barely opened fire, though one young man was cut to pieces by bursts from a machine gun and two others were crushed by tanks. By the 21st the showdown was over, the putschists defeated. Russia had won. Gorbachev returned to the presidency of a country that was fast ceasing to exist.

In the seventies the Serbsky Institute had won infamy and ostracism for allowing its psychiatrists to prescribe pharmaceuticals to punish dissidents, some of whom had been strong enough to resist, though others had been chemically lobotomized. Now, like many other Soviet institutions, it was making the attempt to become "normal," the catchword of the day, one that reflected more hope than experience.

Chikatilo was always glad to go over the story of his life one more time, especially in that institute which could help save his life by declaring him insane. He stressed the horrors of his childhood, the war, the bombs, the bodies; and, even worse— his older brother, Stepan, cannibalized in the great famine of the thirties. No documents, however, could be found concerning the birth of a Stepan Chikatilo and the people from his village did not remember any such boy. Still, Chikatilo's own sister, Tanya, had testified that his mother had told him that story over and over again in his childhood, weeping as she spoke.

It may have been the truth, or Chikatilo's mother may only have used the story to make him wary of strangers during the famine after the war. In either case, it became part of Chikatilo's fantasy life, like being a partisan in the woods. As he said of himself: "I fantasized my whole life and sometimes couldn't tell my fantasies from reality."

He spoke freely of his fantasy life, but discussed his murders "calmly and coldly," as the report would note. He made formal statements of contrition when he remembered to, which was not often. From time to time he would, however, make interesting revelations—that he had used his fingers or his knife to place his semen in the anus or vagina of his victims to make it appear that "normal sex" had occurred. The slitting open of a belly had caused him a second and immediate ejaculation.

In everything he said or wrote, Chikatilo presented himself as a "poisoned wolf," a man infuriated by impotence which avenged itself on the genitals of his victims. Chikatilo saw himself as a person "of extremes, whose aspirations were too great and so whose fall was very low."

The psychiatrists of the Serbsky Institute, however, viewed him as a cautious sadist with no derangements that would prevent him from knowing his acts were wrongful, acts that had been premeditated and not in the least the result of chance and sudden overwhelming need. On October 25, 1991, the Institute issued its findings, choosing block letters for the words that mattered most: LEGALLY SANE.

Chikatilo was stunned as he read the findings and came to those words in capital letters.

"I can't face the trial, I'll hang myself," said Chikatilo to

Kostoev, who had waited as Chikatilo read the nineteen-page single-spaced report in Butyrki Prison in Moscow where he was being held pending his return to Rostov.

"It's the court that decides, not the Serbsky Institute," said Kostoev, who wanted Chikatilo alive and lucid for the trial. "Just tell the truth in your testimony, and the court will weigh everything. Only the court has the authority to pass judgment on the legal sanity of a defendant."

"I want to read the indictment again," Chikatilo demanded. Kostoev had been able to give him a copy of the indictment, nearly complete except for the findings of the Serbsky Institute and Kostoev's finishing touches on his own personality analysis of Chikatilo. In early November the Supreme Court of Russia had overturned Alexander Kravchenko's death sentence, and Kostoev had been able to include Chikatilo's first murder in the indictment. The battle between the Attorney General and the courts had lasted from January to November, but the evidence had been too clear, too strong, and, since the coup, there had been a shift in society toward a greater respect for the law. Chikatilo had been able to acquaint himself with that long document in which he was charged with fifty-three of the fifty-five murders to which he had confessed, two bodies never having been found. There were also five counts of child molestation.

"No," said Kostoev, "you already told me you've read it three times. That's enough. It's time for us to say goodbye, Andrei Romanovich."

Kostoev could see how unwilling Chikatilo was to leave this phase of his life in which he had been the object of great attention, well-fed, supplied with newspapers, receiving notes from his wife. Soon he would be in public, in a courtroom, having to face the parents of the children he had killed.

"I'll be sending you back to Rostov in a couple of days," said Kostoev. "You'll be in that same KGB isolation prison, it's the safest place for you. If you have any requests, inform KGB officer Ermolenko and he'll call me.

"I'll tell Fenya to send her letters and packages there, they'll get through to you, don't worry.

"One other thing, Andrei Romanovich, I'll be fully aware of how you act at the trial, and so my advice to you is—be smart."

As they shook hands in a last farewell in Butyrki Prison in Moscow, Chikatilo grew a little misty-eyed. Compassion was not dead in him, thought Kostoev, he still had some for himself.

The overturning of Kravchenko's death sentence had been a great victory for Kostoev and all the investigators involved, but it also created the painful task of informing Kravchenko's mother that her son's execution had now been judged wrongful.

Kostoev felt that he and the other people still working on his team were too emotionally involved to assume the task.

Kostoev called his secretary and asked: "Is there anyone from Ukraine working here with us in Moscow?"

"Yes, there is," she replied, "Sergei Grebenshchikov."

"Put me through to him," said Kostoev, waiting through the clicks and static for the voice which finally identified itself as Sergei Grebenshchikov.

"How long since you've been home?" asked Kostoev.

"Quite a while."

"I can get you a few days at home if you'll do a favor for me on the way."

"Sounds good to me. I'll come to your office and we can discuss the details."

Tall, blond, gray-eyed, Grebenshchikov had a good reputation as an investigator and quickly grasped the essentials of the Kravchenko case: The son was executed in 1983 and now the mother must be informed that the Russian Supreme Court had overturned the sentence. Kostoev also instructed him to see if the mother could provide any interesting information on her son's behavior after his arrest.

Kravchenko's mother, Maria, was a sixty-three-year-old country woman who looked much older than her years. Very simple by nature, she had received only a fourth-grade education. There was little she could tell Grebenshchikov about her son's behavior after his arrest for the murder of the little girl in Shakhty. He had just kept saying, "I didn't do it."

"I haven't heard any news from him for quite some time now," Maria Kravchenko told Grebenshchikov. "And when I dream that it's raining or snowing, I start to worry about him."

"I'm here to inform you," said Grebenshchikov, beginning to suspect the unthinkable—that no one had even informed the mother of her son's execution—"that the sentence passed against your son has been overturned by the Russian Federation Supreme Court."

"And my boy," asked Maria Kravchenko, smiling faintly at the abstractions, "where is he now?"

CHAPTER 25

By the time Chikatilo had been remanded back to Rostov, the Soviet Union had ceased to exist. The statue of the founder of the secret police had been toppled from its pedestal in front of KGB headquarters in Moscow, and the white-, blue-, and red-striped flag of a new Russia now flew over the Kremlin.

In Rostov a plush gambling casino opened at once, springing full blown into life as if it had been waiting patiently for decades. On the streets, people at card tables sold champagne and shampoo. Scratch cards with images of icons of the Virgin promised winners instant rubles and, for the luckiest of all, a Citroën. Homegrown pornography sent up its first shoots in the rainy April of 1992 when everything in Rostov, and Russia, seemed a gamble.

The courthouse where Chikatilo's trial was about to begin on April 14, 1992, was an imposing municipal edifice whose pastel peach walls and brickwork were offset by its many white columns and arches. It did have the misfortune of being located next to the Musical Comedy Theater, which had been under construction for almost twenty years and was not even close to being half done, the cranes idled, the project abandoned like communism itself, a sense of wild neglect everywhere.

Inside the courthouse, the walls were also peach-colored but tinged with more red than the yellowish exterior. The many clocks in the building had all stopped at 1:29. When this was brought to Judge Akubzhanov's attention by a foreign correspondent, the judge said, with the exasperation of those explaining the elementary: "What do you expect, this is Russia."

A thin, dark-haired chain-smoker, Akubzhanov vibrated with high nervous energy. He would be in charge of the three-man panel that would decide Chikatilo's fate. It was an enormous burden, 225 volumes of evidence, the media in from every country, and great pressure to conduct this trial as it would be done in the "civilized world," the new Russian buzz-word for Europe, America.

Many people were waiting in the vast vestibule in front of Courtroom 5 on April 14, 1992. The eight-foot doors to the courtroom, still closed, were flanked by tall crimson plaques emblazoned with golden letters:

IN EVERYTHING IT DOES THE COURT EDUCATES CITIZENS OF THE SOVIET UNION IN A SPIRIT OF DEVOTION TO THE MOTHERLAND AND THE CAUSE OF COMMUNISM, IN A SPIRIT OF EXACT AND UNDEVIATING FULFILLMENT OF SOVIET LAWS.

The parents and relatives of the victims stood off to the sides, in little groups. Around each face was an aura of raw grief and wrath, the lips of some of the men bitter with a tragedy for which there can be no justice or solace.

There was a stir of anticipation, then a hush as the doors to the courtroom were opened. The relatives of victims to sit on the benches to the left; everyone else on the right. Carrying volumes of evidence under their arms, the three judges marched through the courtroom to the raised dais where they would sit on chairs into whose oversized wooden backs hammers and sickles had been carved.

Then, to the accompaniment of groans and curses from the

relatives of victims, Chikatilo was hustled by Internal Forces troops up the staircase at the right side of the courtroom, and into the iron cage built to protect murderers from attack. Chikatilo's head had been shaved, standard procedure against lice, all that bare shining skin only making him look all the more maniacal. He was wearing a shirt with the 1980 Moscow Olympics insignia, the boycotted, poisoned Olympics. Chikatilo would wear that shirt every day of his six-month trial.

The opening sessions were devoted to a reading of the charges, which elicited shrieks and threats.

Except for their commander, the Internal Forces troops guarding Chikatilo were in their late teens or very early twenties, a few sporting a first thin mustache. As Judge Akubzhanov read the charges, one of those young men in the khaki uniforms with crimson epaulettes turned pale and sank slowly down into a chair.

For a week Chikatilo listened in silence as the charges were read and screams of hatred hurled at him. Then, on April 21, he announced, "I'm guilty of all the murders except the first, Lena Zakotnova."

Kostoev was furious. He had no doubt a deal had been struck between the Rostov authorities and Chikatilo, who'd been told something like: After the trial, no matter what the verdict, you're going to be in the Rostov prison system for quite a while. That can be a good period or it can be a bad period, it all depends on you. Forget that first murder, what's the difference, fifty-two or fifty-three?

Kostoev knew from old experience how all the elements of the Rostov justice system could come together to defend themselves. If Chikatilo was not convicted of that murder along with the rest when the verdict was read, Kostoev would launch an immediate investigation, and it would even take precedence over looking into just exactly what went wrong in 1984 when confessions were being wrung from half-wits in Rostov and Chikatilo was being arrested and let free.

Chikatilo was represented in court by a young and intelligent lawyer, Marat Khabibulin, who looked and dressed like an English don. He sat at a desk in front of Chikatilo's cage, facing the State Prosecutor, who wore a uniform of blue and gold and who stood on the same side of the courtroom as the victims' relatives. Khabibulin took his responsibilities seriously, out of respect for the principle that guilt had to be proved in a court of law. And to defend a man like Chikatilo made for an interesting professional and moral challenge, to say the least.

In the beginning Chikatilo testified openly if flatly about the details of his crimes. "I would just invite them to come with me, and then I'd start walking away and sometimes they'd come walking after me."

As he spoke, a woman screamed and fainted at the thought of her daughter walking off behind that man. First aid was summoned, two morose young women in dingy smocks carrying huge hypodermics.

The press snapped photographs. It was a big story, the local papers had already started calling it the "trial of the century" for the "crime of the century." Readers sent letters to the editor suggesting fit punishments for such a "monster." One man, who preferred anonymity, proposed that Chikatilo "either be burned at the stake or lashed to death in a public ceremony that would be broadcast on television to all Russia. The relatives would be allowed ten blows each but the remainder should be administered by those true sons of Russia, the Cossacks!"

Chikatilo's appetite for newspapers was still being fed by the authorities to ensure his cooperation, though some columnists were later to ask whether it was acceptable practice for the defendant to be aware of his coverage in the media. In any case, Chikatilo himself was of the opinion that, both in the courtroom and in the press, he was being treated as if his guilt had been established beyond doubt.

On April 29, Chikatilo shocked the court by announcing that

his presumption of innocence had been irredeemably violated. "I am calling for a new trial," said Chikatilo, his voice muffled and hollow in the sound system which distorted as much as it amplified. "This trial has violated my rights. The judge already considers me guilty and has said so many times. And that has been picked up by the press. . . . I think that the court has already concluded I am guilty and my fate has already been determined. And, for that reason, I will give no further testimony."

Chikatilo lapsed into immediate silence. Judge Akubzhanov continued his questioning. But Chikatilo would not respond to the judge, the prosecutor, or even his own defense attorney. There was something hostile about the profundity of that silence that enraged the parents of some victims even more than his testimony.

"Say something, Chikatilo!" screamed a blonde woman, leaping to her feet. "Say something, you bastard!"

But Chikatilo did not react to her in the slightest, either totally distracted or enjoying the suffering he could still inflict.

Then it was the prosecutor who outraged the court by stating that he supported Chikatilo in part, saying the judges had made too many rash remarks about Chikatilo's guilt. Now people were on their feet, screaming, demanding that the prosecutor be replaced. The trial had to be interrupted again. Judge Akubzhanov and his two assistants, known as People's Assessors, retired to discuss two issues: whether they should be replaced or the prosecutor.

Back in the courtroom their announcement—the Court will stay, the prosecutor will go—was greeted by applause from the benches where the victims' families sat. The trial proceeded for a few days without the prosecution being represented, until a clamor was raised by the judicial community and the press—it was unthinkable for a trial to proceed without the prosecution being represented. A new prosecutor was immediately appointed, in fact with such speed that only afterward was it learned that the official in question had already left on a six-week vacation, prompting *Izvestiya* to ask if it wouldn't have been too much to first find out if the man was even available. The trial went into recess until a replacement for the prosecutor could be found.

"It's a circus, not a trial!" shouted one of the victims' relatives in the foyer after the trial had been recessed for the indefinite future, the judges walking out first with the volumes of evidence under their arms, Chikatilo whisked down the stairs by the Internal Forces troops, his expression gleeful.

Following the trial closely from Moscow, Kostoev was disgusted with what he'd heard. Psychological contact with Chikatilo had been lost. He was vastly amused, if equally disgusted, by another scandal connected with the trial, though not directly. The psychiatrist, Alexander Olympievich Bukhanovsky, whom Kostoev had called in on the ninth day of interrogation to assure Chikatilo that there was genuine medical interest in his case, was now claiming credit for "cracking the killer" and had extended his duly recorded hour and a half with Chikatilo to something like eight.

"I spoke with Chikatilo for nearly an entire day. It was then—for the first time in his life—that he spoke aloud of the terrible crimes he had on his conscience. . . . After that conversation, I came out and said—'Yes, that's the man and I think he'll speak to you now.' " Bukhanovsky was also claiming that he had drawn up a psychological profile of the killer five years earlier that proved remarkably accurate.

Kostoev fired back in an interview with the Moscow edition of *Pravda* on May 14, 1992: "There are people who are pursuing their own selfish interests, I'm thinking of a certain Bukhanovsky in particular. Now he's founded his own association, Phoenix, which consults on apprehending criminals. He's stated that he drew a portrait of the killer five years ago. But there's no such document in all the three hundred volumes of evidence."

But not all the news was shocking and unpleasant. Finally, as a result of his capturing and cracking Chikatilo, Issa Kostoev was, on May 12, 1992, by presidential decree, promoted from Colonel to General, every rank in the Justice Department having its military equivalent. The glory had a bitter taste as well, for he knew that if he had not been an Ingush he would not have had to wait seventeen years to fulfill the boast and oath he had made when he and Asya were first married: "We'll live in Moscow and I'll be a general."

The irony was that no sooner had he reached the top of his profession than he might be deprived of it. His countrymen were importuning him, as the only Ingush general, to become their political leader and fight for the return of their ancestral lands. So far, Kostoev had been able to resist the temptations of honor.

A new rumor swept Rostov—the Japanese were offering to pay a fortune for Chikatilo's brain. There was no basis to that rumor, but both in the press and in private discussion many people did indeed favor Chikatilo's remaining alive to be studied. Others held that death was the only justice for such a killer. Chikatilo's deeds made a strong case for those who favored capital punishment; but the fact that for his very first murder another man had been wrongfully executed lent support to those who opposed the death penalty. Either side could use Chikatilo, forever the doubler.

The trial proceeded by jolts and breaks. Someone threw a hundred grams of mercury into one of Courtroom 5's open windows. The court had to be cleared and a recess announced until the room could be decontaminated and properly secured.

Other disruptions were caused by the new strategy Chikatilo had adopted. He now declared that he had remembered four other murders but was recanting on six to which he had already confessed. "They're only going to come back gradually to me," said Chikatilo. "I even wrote to the Russian Attorney General that I might have killed seventy."

It was clear to the court that Chikatilo was only fighting to buy himself time. The new murders would require new investigations and that would take months. Time was the only thing left to fight for, and Chikatilo was fighting.

But then his aggressive attempts to disrupt the trial were transformed into suicidal litanies: "I've caused a lot of grief. It's time to be rid of me. I want to speed up the trial." Then, for a time, the trial proceeded with stately tranquillity. People who had worked with Chikatilo were now giving testimony. They all said they had no idea that this man, neither friendly nor a particularly good worker, was the maniac of Rostov. It was striking how little they all could remember of a man they worked with side by side for years. Chikatilo had made no impression at all, and now, to their horror, they understood why.

Having failed to obstruct the proceedings, Chikatilo switched course again and began complaining of nightmares, hallucinations, insomnia. He was convinced that the KGB was bombarding him with some sort of rays. He demanded an interpreter, someone who spoke both Ukrainian, Chikatilo's native language, and Abyssinian, a racial insult directed at Judge Akubzhanov, whose name and dark coloring both suggested Eastern origins. Chikatilo began speaking in Ukrainian, calling out, "Long live a free Ukraine!" and even started growing a Ukrainian-style walrus mustache.

"The police should be on trial with me too for letting it all happen!" announced Chikatilo, raising a point that could only be painful to the Rostov police. Chikatilo's remarks made headlines in the Rostov papers, which also clucked over Chikatilo's professed preference of *Pravda* and *Izvestiya* to the newspaper *Evening Rostov*. Chikatilo came alive when cameras were around his cage or when he saw the press taking notes. The media liked Chikatilo, Chikatilo liked the media. Fame is a killer's last crime.

"I am not a homosexual!" screamed Chikatilo at one session, dropping his pants in the iron cage, having removed his underwear earlier in the cell. Hustled away, he was banned from court for several days.

"I have milk in my breasts, I'm going to give birth," announced Chikatilo upon his return, causing a sensation in the courtroom, the press, the country.

Five minutes alone with him, thought Kostoev, and Chikatilo would stop that nonsense, which might even have been unwittingly suggested to him by that specialist in transsexualism and self-aggrandizement, Alexander Olympievich Bukhanovsky.

It was clear to Kostoev that Chikatilo, having done everything he could to obstruct and disrupt the trial and to cast doubts on its impartiality, was now playing the role of madman to the hilt.

Kostoev's worst fears about the trial had been realized. It had not been, in his opinion, conducted with due gravity and respect for judicial process. He made no secret of his opinion, stating it quite clearly in the same interview in which he lambasted Bukhanovsky. In conclusion, the journalist asked:

"Are you saying that Chikatilo's trial, like the 1905 war with Japan that bared all of tsarism's ills, reveals the many ulcerations in our justice system and society?"

"Something like that," replied Kostoev.

It was August in the Caucasus and Kostoev had turned fifty, that fateful age, half of the hundred few ever live to, even in those mountains. The weather was perfect and in the evenings the men dined on lamb in the courtyard, drinking cognac under the stars.

Those were beautiful days for Kostoev but their beauty was shadowed by the tensions now flaring at the border between

Ingushetia and Ossetia. There had already been incidents, shootings, deaths.

Yandiev was against Kostoev's playing any political role and told him so: "Issa, you're a general now, you were born to command. But politics is one compromise after another, it's not for you."

As always, Yandiev's logic was good, but there was another logic operative as well, one Kostoev recognized from his own work where he termed it the "logic of life." It said to Kostoev that his passion for justice derived from the wound of injustice inflicted on his people. Now that that passion had propelled him to the rank of General, justice required that he complete the circle, pay his debt, temporarily sacrifice profession for nation.

Wearing a blue tracksuit with white trim, smoking heavily again, Kostoev paced the compound-like courtyard enclosed by high brick walls, oblivious to the bleatings of lambs in nearby pens or the ringing of hammers one house away. He paused by the evergreen tree around which a bed of roses had been planted, as strange a combination of north and south as his own life.

Alright, alright, he'd do it, six months, a year at most.

"Arise, ye prisoners of starvation," sang Andrei Chikatilo in the Rostov court, the anthem of international communism hollowed by his voice reverberating in the bars. "There will be one last, decisive battle!"

And there was indeed: that same day, August 14, 1992, the prosecution asked for death on all fifty-three counts of premeditated murder. The state's position remained that Andrei Chikatilo was a sadist who tortured and murdered for his own sexual pleasure. He was a cunning and knowing criminal who took every possible precaution to cover his trail, never leaving a single clue at the scene of a crime. Chikatilo had also demonstrated the ability to refrain from murdering when he felt his own life was in danger, as was evident from his behavior after his first murder in 1978. And, when Rostov province was no longer open to him after 1984, he shifted his venues and his modus operandi, killing people all over the Soviet Union. Records demonstrated that Chikatilo, from 1978 on, always had access to a house or apartment where he could count on being alone, if only to clean or change his clothing. And in nineteen cases of murder, the hard, material evidence had been supplied by Chikatilo himself. Though Chikatilo obviously suffered from a number of mental derangements, he both knew the difference between right and wrong, and was able to resist his impulses when it was to his benefit to do so. And thus, by the internationally accepted definition, Chikatilo was legally sane.

"There is no question that Chikatilo could tell right from wrong," responded Marat Khabibulin, Chikatilo's defense attorney, when making his final plea, speaking for an hour and a half without notes. "What remains unclear medically is whether or not he was able to control his actions. There should have been independent psychiatric evaluation of Chikatilo. The Serbsky Institute is an official institution of the same state that is prosecuting Chikatilo. And the ethical reputation of the Serbsky Institute is not without blemish. At one time it was used for political, not psychiatric, purposes. I am thinking of those cases in which people who were perfectly healthy mentally were declared insane. In other words, the Institute did the bidding of society. And where is the guarantee that, under the pressure of public opinion, the Serbsky Institute has not now declared an insane man to be of sound mind."

The last word was offered to Chikatilo but he slouched in his cage, still wearing the Olympic shirt, and said nothing, silence his final response.

After taking two months to write the verdict, Judge Akubzhanov set October 14, 1992, as the date when sentencing would begin. First, the list of crimes would have to be recited one last time. Shrieks began filling the courtroom, even keener for being the last in the murderer's presence. The wild cries continued into the next day when the list of fifty-two murders was completed, one having been dropped for insufficient evidence, but it was not the killing of his first victim, the nine-year-old schoolgirl, Lena Zakotnova.

Judge Akubzhanov spoke of the Soviet Union's refusal to acknowledge crime in its midst, which had contributed to these tragedies, as had the Soviet practice of obedience which had caused so many children to follow that teacherly man into the woods.

The cries subsided to moans, then rose again as Judge Akubzhanov read the sentence:

"Irrespective of any mitigating circumstances, and, considering the extraordinary cruelty of the crimes, the court cannot but give Andrei Romanovich Chikatilo the only punishment he deserves, the supreme penalty—the court sentences him to death!"

Pandemonium broke out. Chikatilo began ranting. Applauding spectators climbed up onto the benches as cameramen rushed Chikatilo's cage, where they were rebuffed by guards. Someone hurled a chunk of metal at Chikatilo, bouncing resoundingly off the bars of his cage.

"Chikatilo," said Judge Akubzhanov, "you are sentenced to death, do you understand?"

"Swindlers! I fought for a free Russia and a free Ukraine!" shouted Chikatilo. "Swindlers!"

His defense attorney declared his intention to appeal the verdict to the Supreme Court of Russia and, if turned down there, as a final resort, to address a plea for clemency directly to President Yeltsin.

The shrieks and keening reached a crescendo as Judge Akubzhanov instructed the head of the guard: "Take Chikatilo from the courtroom."

As the cage door was opened for the last time, a woman

whose twelve-year-old son was murdered by Chikatilo rushed at him only to be stopped by three of the guards. There were cries of outrage amidst the sobbing and applause. Some parents were standing and shouting, tormented by the knowledge that justice had been done but could never be done, for if justice was to satisfy both mind and emotion, it would have to grant their hearts' desire, which they had screamed at the beginning of that trial and were still screaming now: "GIVE HIM TO US SO WE CAN TEAR HIM TO PIECES LIKE HE DID TO OUR CHILDREN!"

EPILOGUE

In prison Chikatilo reverted to the pen. And to his favorite genre, the letter of complaint.

Xeroxes of Chikatilo's letters to the Russian Attorney General went immediately to Kostoev, who read them with revulsion, amusement, fascination.

The letters varied but their point was always the same—Chikatilo was a victim too.

The victim of communism. "I gave 40 years of my life to the building of communism and for 25 years I was a militant member of the Communist Party with an iron faith in the Worldwide Victory of Communism. . . . I dreamed of becoming the leader of the Soviet Union.

"I am a victim of that criminal, inhuman system, of the famines Stalin organized in Ukraine in 1933 and 1947 that resulted in millions of deaths and cases of cannibalism. I am a victim of Stalin's injustices, of the serf-like conditions on collective farms, and of the Brezhnev years of stagnation. I am a victim of the Bolshevik experiment—the crimes I committed coincide in time with the years of criminal war in Afghanistan.

"How is anyone supposed to stay normal after all that?

"Thank God for the end of that system and its murderers, monsters, and criminals."

Kostoev saw that the collapse of communism had given

Chikatilo a new argument, as it had everyone else in the country who now sought to justify their felonies and corruption. Kostoev hated them for not even having the courage of common criminals, claiming instead that only the system had inhibited their inherent nobility.

Chikatilo's statements were riddled with inconsistencies. Chikatilo's crimes did not coincide with the Afghan War but preceded it by eleven years. And when he stressed how unsparingly he had given of himself to communism—"I never took a single vacation or had medical treatment at a sanatorium"—his words, though true in themselves, actually only screened the corpses of the people Chikatilo had killed in 1982 while he was supposed to be receiving treatment for his arthritis.

Tens of millions suffered under Stalin. Kostoev suffered under Stalin. No proof had ever been found that Chikatilo had a brother or that he had been abducted, killed, and eaten. But Kostoev had two brothers and a sister who had all died in a single month during the Kazakhstan exile. The system could be blamed for the harm it inflicted, but not for the harm a person inflicted in turn.

Chikatilo was not only the victim of the communist system but of his own "nervous system which had collapsed. In depair, suffering fits of fury, nervous exhaustion and mental breakdown, I attacked my innocent victims who were themselves hostages to a perverted and monstrous system of genocide."

Chikatilo even blamed his own blood, quoting an article from *Izvestiya:* "In the opinion of certain foreign scientists, a person's character, temperament, and health depend on his blood type. It is thought those with type AB possess at least two souls."

Kostoev had to agree with that. Chikatilo did have two souls. And he might even have been born with them. But it was murder, not nature, that made that second soul separate and distinct.

The only other note of sincerity Kostoev detected was in Chikatilo's harangue about the "mafia that had blocked the windows of my son's poor home with outdoor toilets and private garages"—on that subject he truly was crazy.

Going so far even as to present himself as the victim of religious persecution, Chikatilo wrote that he and his family had been "mercilessly humiliated, poisoned, and beaten" for attempting to attend church. And now he requested that no less a person than the "Patriarch of All the Russians, the Most Holy Alexei II, permit me to make my confession to God for the sins I have committed."

But it wasn't only communism, nerves, and blood that were at fault, it was people, mean and spiteful. "At work when I tried to do my best, I was constantly fired and driven from my home, torn from life and hurled into stations, trains, and forest strips."

But everything Chikatilo said or did was clearly a move to save his own life, or prolong it, his most basic instinct, survival, remaining healthy and intact.

Kostoev was not deceived. In all Chikatilo's complaints he saw only cruelty, the robbing of the people he had killed of the last thing they had left, the uniqueness of their victimhood.

But Kostoev had not finally come to know Chikatilo until the day Chikatilo told him a story.

"They took me to showers this morning. There were a lot of us there. One of the other prisoners was walking around and boasting: 'I'm in for knocking off five.'

"I didn't say anything to him. How would he have felt if I'd said I was in for 55?" said Chikatilo, laughing with gusto and abandon at the etiquette of homicide.

Only then did Kostoev see who Chikatilo was. At the core. Beneath the mask of grandfather, the mask of communist, the mask of the insulted and injured, the final mask of derangement.

And what Kostoev saw was the arrogance of self-pity. The vengeance of which weakness dreams. Abdication of everything human as impediment. Surrender to the might of evil, mysterious as God and death, real as the wounds in a child's flesh.

INDEX